UNITING
Mind, Body, Spirit

UNITING
Mind, Body, Spirit

Science and the Spiritual Exercises of St. Ignatius

Roy Pereira, SJ

Paulist Press
New York / Mahwah, NJ

Scripture quotations are from New Revised Standard Version Bible: Catholic Edition, copyright © 1989, 1993 National Council of the Churches of Christ in the United States of America. Used by permission. All rights reserved worldwide.

Cover photo by Annie Spratt on Unsplash
Cover design by Joe Gallagher
Book design by Lynn Else

Copyright © 2024 by Dr. Roy Pereira, SJ

All rights reserved. No part of this publication may be reproduced, stored in a retrieval system, or transmitted in any form or by any means, electronic, mechanical, photocopying, recording, scanning, or otherwise, without either the prior written permission of the Publisher, or authorization through payment of the appropriate per-copy fee to the Copyright Clearance Center, Inc., www.copyright.com. Requests to the Publisher for permission should be addressed to the Permissions Department, Paulist Press, permissions@paulistpress.com.

Library of Congress Cataloging-in-Publication Data
Names: Pereira, Roy, author.
Title: Uniting mind, body, spirit: science and the spiritual exercises of St. Ignatius / Roy Pereira, SJ ; foreword by Arturo Sosa, SJ.
Description: Paperback. | New York ; Mahwah, NJ : Paulist Press, [2024] | Includes bibliographical references and index. | Summary: "The book combines recent research from neuroscience as well as the rich insights of Ignatian spirituality to produce a wealth of strategies for living abundantly and well during challenging times"—Provided by publisher.
Identifiers: LCCN 2023030660 (print) | LCCN 2023030661 (ebook) | ISBN 9780809154852 (paperback) | ISBN 9781587688812 (ebook)
Subjects: LCSH: Ignatius, of Loyola, Saint, 1491–1556. Exercitia spiritualia. | Spiritual exercises.
Classification: LCC BX2353 .P38 2024 (print) | LCC BX2353 (ebook) | DDC 248.3—dc23/eng/20231130
LC record available at https://lccn.loc.gov/2023030660
LC ebook record available at https://lccn.loc.gov/2023030661

ISBN 978-0-8091-5485-2 (paperback)
ISBN 978-1-58768-881-2 (e-book)

Published by Paulist Press
997 Macarthur Boulevard
Mahwah, New Jersey 07430
www.paulistpress.com

Printed and bound in the
United States of America

To all the readers/listeners of this book

To all the faculty/staff/students in universities around the world (Jesuit and others) especially my students who have listened to me, challenged me, and helped me grow

To all my future audience in academia, parishes, and people across the globe

To my benefactors, and above all to God

CONTENTS

Foreword ix

Preface xi

Acknowledgments xiii

Introduction xv

Chapter 1. Uncertainty, Rapid Change, and Ignatius 1

Chapter 2. Health and Healing 10

Chapter 3. Decision-Making: A Leap of Faith? 21

Chapter 4. Brain and Behavior Change 31

Chapter 5. Journey toward Mindfulness 48

Chapter 6. Let's Grow Together: Further Ignatian Insights 60

Notes 71

Bibliography 79

Index 87

About the Author 89

FOREWORD

THROUGH THIS BOOK, Fr. Roy Pereira, SJ, desires to reach a larger universe of people who can benefit from his practical methods for spreading positive attitudes and feeling good. Pereira's proposals constitute a kind of "first aid kit" for those who feel their hearts are wounded and in need of healing and strength. More importantly, he proposes a process that focuses on the common welfare rather than on the individual. Healing the wounds of the heart is only possible by giving oneself to others and contributing to the creation of a community based on healthy and healing relationships.

The great variety of people and their cultural diversity express the richness of the human race. However, there is a common foundation to the diversity and variety that characterize us: our humanity. That substratum of humanity is the greatest help to overcome any crisis. The difficulties that have been accentuated by the crises of recent years are no longer an obstacle to progress toward a better future if we draw nourishment from our roots planted deep in the sustaining substrate that is humanity. From there can emerge a fruitful, enlightened, and enlightening life that does not allow itself to be carried away by discrimination based on ethnic, caste, religious, gender, or cultural differences.

By becoming aware of the immense benefits of having faith, of sharing, of caring, and of loving, we can change the world we live in. Many people, groups, movements, and organizations spread these values and contribute to the awareness of them within themselves, and they invite others to participate in these

UNITING MIND, BODY, SPIRIT

values as well. They each contribute their grain of sand to overcome the current crises and to build a better world.

In this book, Fr. Roy Pereira brings together the ideas of neuroscientific research and the teachings of St. Ignatius, weaving an integrative approach to learning, behavior change, decision-making, and mindfulness. The use of QR codes and Pereira's own musical compositions enliven this book. In this original way, he takes advantage of digital advances in the processes of healing hearts and minds. Its scope expands in an almost unimaginable way.

I hope that the dissemination of this book into our vast world will become a powerful instrument to heal wounded hearts, change behavior, and engage in the transformation of social relations, allowing humanity to prevail.

Arturo Sosa, SJ
Superior General of the Society of Jesus
Rome, July 11, 2022

PREFACE

IT IS EXCITING TO see your thoughts appear as words on paper. I have had years of opportunities to speak my thoughts to a wide range of groups in an academic setting, in a pastoral setting, and to youth in over ten countries. I have published academic papers, edited a journal and a book, but this project is a synthesis of my subject of neuroscience and the spirituality of the Jesuits, where I have spent a major portion of my life. While there have been many downsides to the pandemic, one benefit for me was the time that I suddenly had on my hands to sit down and write. For a teacher or a preacher, speaking in public is easy and gives immediate gratification. The rigor and discipline of writing is a whole other story.

I have given a number of presentations on such uncertain times and how it has an effect on our health, psyche, and spirit. While, for a time, the uncertainty of COVID-19 loomed large in the foreground, there are still many other challenges in the world today that are more difficult to solve and will not go away in a hurry. Almost one hundred years ago, Charlie Chaplin presented to us the difficulties of modern life in his iconic film *Modern Times*. We continue to be enmeshed in a complicated web of uncertainty, rapid change, and difficulties in this new century. Health has been a repetitive motif in my life beginning with taking it for granted in my youth, neglecting it during my adult life, and now appreciating that the gift of health is precious and the foundation upon which our dreams and goals can take wings. *Faith*, a word with multiple understandings, has anchored me during the times I did not give it a second thought. The riches of Ignatian spirituality have helped deepen and nourish this faith. While my initial studies were in chemistry, my fascination with the mind and the brain that houses it led to my continued love affair with neuroscience. The ability to share this new and exciting field with students at the Creighton School of Medicine and St. Xavier's College, Mumbai, for over a decade has been a fulfilling experience. Many of those students are now pursuing their own careers in neuroscience in various parts of the world. When a hardcore physics student decides to make a shift to neuroscience, the beauty of this interdisciplinary subject gratifies me. Thus, seeking to bring together neuroscience and Ignatian spirituality seems a logical milestone in my academic and life journey.

ACKNOWLEDGMENTS

I AM GRATEFUL to the hundreds of students in my classroom, the AICUF, and the varied audiences across numerous cities on different continents (and more recently, even virtual assemblies, especially the Saturday Vigil Mass Group) that have listened to my talks and have also challenged me with their curiosity. I am also grateful to the Society of Jesus, which has been my home for thirty-six years and the wonderful fellow Jesuits that I have encountered in various provinces. For this book in particular, I am grateful to the following reviewers: Paul Coutinho, Richard Howard, Vincent Murphy, and Lyle Michael. I am grateful to Michael Kennedy and his team at Jesuit Restorative Justice Initiative, especially Monica Tenorio. I thank Joseph Aloysius for designing the original cover page. Thanks also to Sneha, Daniel, and Sanjay Noronha, Amelia Casado-Fuente, Ronnie and Jeanette Dalgado. I also thank Fr. Don Doll, SJ, of Creighton University for the profile photographs. I am also thankful to Eduardo Fernandez, Michael Garanzini, Edward Siebert, and the Jesuit community at Loyola Marymount University (LMU) and to Kawanna Leggett, Terri Mangione, Francesca Piumutti, Rich Rochleau, and Lane Bove.

If there has been someone who has walked with me from the start of this book to its culmination, it has been my graduate assistant, Harshad Parekar. I am immensely grateful for our regular conversations and his ability to be a good sounding board that has made this a much better book.

UNITING MIND, BODY, SPIRIT

Finally, I am grateful to my Jesuit family, my sisters, and the inspiration that my mum and dad continue to provide from the beyond; my mum, Arlene, for the musical talent instilled in me and my dad, Richard, for being a living example of how to harness the power of the mind.

INTRODUCTION

"AM I AUDIBLE? Can I be seen?"

These two questions heard perennially on a Zoom call are micro-expressions of the uncertain times we are going through. The first casualty of living in such times is our health. The second consequence is that we become paralyzed and unable to act.

Rapidly changing situations go hand in hand with uncertain times and call for a change in our behavior patterns if we are to continue to remain relevant. An important tool for behavior change is mindfulness. With the help of Ignatian insights, we can better navigate these times. Throughout this book, several practical steps are provided in each chapter to facilitate a life of abundance (John 10:10) and self-healing.

The book begins by laying out a picture of the uncertain times we are in. It also points out that although these are undefined and difficult times, these are not unprecedented times. Related to uncertainty is the rapid change we experience in things, big or small. The original meaning of "zoom" has been overshadowed to now mean the ubiquitous software program, Zoom, that we use to communicate in classrooms and workplaces, and even for social interaction. Praying together is no longer a physical space phenomenon. The way we shop, exchange money, and even entertain ourselves has taken on new dimensions. It is something we had seen only in space-age movies. We then get into our time machine and travel back five hundred years to the time of Ignatius and the uncertain times he grew up in. The sixteenth century was a time of immense upheavals as humanity slowly moved from the Dark Ages through the Renaissance, the Scientific Revolution, and finally to the period of the Enlightenment in the following centuries.

After mapping out the uncertain times in the first chapter, the second chapter deals with health because such times and rapid change can have a disastrous effect on our health. Health is looked upon as wholeness, complete well-being of mind, body, and spirit. Recent advances in the field of medicine as applied to the human body and brain have been noted. Using the understanding of the brain, as given to us by current neuroscience research, we know that not only does the mind affect the body, but the body in turn affects the brain. This effect is not just psychological but is an actual physical change in the brain. We also learn that all the thoughts in our mind have a direct bearing on the body. Constant negative thinking and emotions of fear, nervousness, and anxiety express themselves in various ways on and within the body. But getting rid of negative thinking is easier said than done. There are multiple ways offered to do this. Nurturing our spiritual selves is also integral to overall health, irrespective of the religion we follow, or maybe don't.

The third chapter tackles a common occurrence during times of crisis or rapid change—the paralysis of action; it also zooms into the heart of the spirituality of St. Ignatius, namely, his Discernment of Spirits. It is helpful to be aware of a method of decision-making that can stand us in good stead during times of uncertainty and doubt. The steps of the process are outlined with examples.

Times of chaos and unpredictability call for a new normal. They call for new ways of behaving, acting, and functioning in the world. So, the fourth chapter deals with behavioral change. In the previous chapter, we went through the process required for discernment and how to choose a particular way of acting amidst a host of competing choices. Having decided what it is that we would want to change in our life, we will then seek how

Introduction

to do it. Our earlier attempt to understand the basic workings of the brain will give us the knowledge to bring about such behavioral change. Besides theory, many practical steps are proposed to help us acquire the new behavior we desire.

One of the steps to bring about behavioral change is the practice of mindfulness, which is dealt with in the fifth chapter. It helps to rearrange old patterns of acting and replace them with new behaviors. Negative emotions generated from thinking about the past (guilt and regret) or thinking about the future (worry and anxiety) can wreak havoc on our immune system. The anticipated outcomes of this chapter include extracting the baggage of the past that we carry in our minds, implanting a new framework of thinking, and allowing this to develop into new patterns of behavior.

Help from Ignatian insights will assist us in achieving these outcomes promptly. But attaining psychological well-being is not enough. We need to go beyond, "I'm okay, and you're okay;" even beyond, "I'm not okay and you're not okay. But that's okay!" Complete human flourishing needs to bring meaning and purpose alongside a feeling of well-being and peace. Why am I here? What is my mission? How can I find happiness? The answers lie in the act of going beyond the self to reach out and offer a helping hand to those in need. Mindfulness and Ignatian insights can help us address broader societal issues of discrimination, unequal access, climate change, and a more just social order.

In the last chapter, we will lay out aspects of Ignatian spirituality that are necessary for everyday living, even more so during uncertain times. These Ignatian aspects are context, freedom, attitude, gratitude, belief, sensitivity, regular review, and the *Magis*. The spirituality of St. Ignatius is a handy guidebook. During difficult times in particular, his Discernment of Spirits has been a method that has stood the test of time. The insights of St. Ignatius along with the findings of recent neuroscience research will help us bring about the behavioral change we wish

UNITING MIND, BODY, SPIRIT

in our lives. But we need to remember that this is a slow process. We need to be patient. The change will come about, but maybe not as fast as we would like it. At all times, we must keep in mind that behavioral change is for the purpose of making a difference in the world. True happiness results from this.

1

UNCERTAINTY, RAPID CHANGE, AND IGNATIUS

SINCE THE SPRING of 2020, we have been in uncertain times. At the start of COVID-19, when the whole world went into lockdown and everyone was wearing masks and practicing social distancing, people would often refer to this period as unprecedented times. It is, in fact, not true! Almost exactly one hundred years ago, the 1918 influenza pandemic hit the whole planet. Also known as the great influenza epidemic, it was caused by the H1N1 influenza A virus. The first case to be recorded was in March of 1918.[1] It was in Kansas, in the United States. Later, in April of 1918, more such cases were recorded in France, Germany, and the United Kingdom. By 1920, one-third of the people in the world had become infected in four successive waves. We do not have the exact figures, but it was approximated that 500 million people became infected. The number of people who succumbed to death was between 25 million to 50 million (the most accepted number). However, other estimates place the death toll from 17.4 to 100 million.[2] If we look at photos from those days, we see everyone in masks and announcements from government authorities asking people to wash their hands often.

UNITING MIND, BODY, SPIRIT

From the above, we see the similarities between the effects of COVID-19 and the H1N1 influenza A virus of 1918. While initially older people were infected, later young adults also succumbed to the disease. Hospitals packed to their capacity and scarce hospital beds, as seen in 2020–21, mirrored similar conditions from 1918 to 1920.[3] Shortages of supplies and food are another similarity. We also see the mention of the six-year climate anomaly. We ourselves in the twenty-first century are experiencing the effects of climate change, whether it be extreme heat in Europe or floods in different parts of the world. Even though the 1918 pandemic played out for around two years, it did come to an end. Victory was achieved over a virus! The lesson for us here is that we should not succumb to "end-of-the-world" scenarios, feelings of helplessness, or depression. Instead, we should continue to do whatever we can to protect ourselves from the infection of the virus while at the same time keeping our hopes and enthusiasm up. So, while there is uncertainty as to when this current pandemic will end, we can be assured that this is not an unprecedented situation.

The next point deals with *change*. Resulting in lockdowns and limited mobility, the pandemic called for change—change in the way we functioned in an office situation, the classroom, or how we meet one another socially. Zoom became a household word along with Google Meet, Microsoft Teams, and a host of other conference platforms. These were used not only in the academic world or in the workplace, but also to watch movies together, play cards, or solve sudoku puzzles online. Even social functions like birthday parties, anniversaries, and baby showers were held virtually. Some of the newest mega-conference platforms can recreate nearly the whole in-person conference experience.[4] For example, after a speaker delivers a talk to a large audience, the attendees can go into smaller breakout rooms and carry on conversations according to their field of interest. There is also the lounge room where people can hang out and seek to

Uncertainty, Rapid Change, and Ignatius

network—the essential part of a conference—beyond listening to an expert giving a lecture. The use of Artificial Intelligence (AI) and simulation takes the experience of meeting an expert in a group to the next level.

The way we buy and consume goods has also changed by a quantum leap, thanks to the pandemic! Electronic goods, household commodities, and health-care products are delivered to our doorstep. Groceries and food can be ordered on an app. Even something as physical as buying a car or choosing a new house, or selecting your partner to settle into that house, can be done mostly online. The way we deal with money has changed so rapidly that one need not keep loose cash around, and neither does one need to visit a bank in person.

The psychological effects of all these changes are varied. We feel excited after meeting our friends and family from across the world with just a click of a button. We experience a sense of relief for not having to commute in rush-hour traffic daily. Our idea of community is no longer people in our local, physical area but one that is formed from across the world in our Zoom room. The ability to access information at the click of a mouse gives us instant gratification. On the other hand, we still miss the camaraderie built around the water cooler in the office. We miss being in the classroom and all the antics that go with it. Watching a movie online, even with friends, does not replace the experience inside a theatre. Physical isolation from family and friends and forced confinement within the home have a depressing effect on our psyche.[5] When forced to live 24/7 within four walls with no avenues for me-time and personal space, the result is raw behavior and sometimes harmful acting-out.

When the pandemic hit, many churches, temples, mosques, and other places of worship shut down. But what was interesting was how quickly religious organizations adapted by using technology to reach into the homes of believers. Being a believer myself, I would like to share my experience here.

UNITING MIND, BODY, SPIRIT

As soon as the churches came under lockdown here in the United States, some people approached me to offer a Mass that weekend for the people in the Boston area. I knew them from my time of doctoral studies there. The next weekend, we had people joining in from Texas and California. By the third weekend, people from Australia and New Zealand had also joined in since it was Sunday morning for them, a time they would reserve for church anyway. In a sense, the closing of the physical churches allowed for each home to become a church. One person took charge of appointing readers. Another person saw to it that different volunteers were available to play instruments and/or sing hymns, while a third looked after the technical aspect of managing the Zoom platform. The participants were also allowed to voice their prayers or petitions during every Mass. Occasionally, through the use of breakout rooms, the congregation would share their perspective on the readings of that day with a much smaller group. They loved this ability to converse and get to know people from around the world. Children and young adults were also encouraged to participate in the readings and the music. It gave them a platform to overcome their shyness and at the same time build up their confidence levels in speaking or singing in public. Beyond all this, the weekly get-together to pray built a spiritual home for people who were forced to be in isolation as a precautionary measure. They experienced emotional support during that one hour, besides having their spiritual needs met. The relief was also in the chitchat that went on in the WhatsApp group during the week. The faith of the people deepened when a lot of prayer intentions were fulfilled, including the healing of a few people who were in a critical condition because of COVID-19. Even though many people now attend an in-person Mass in their respective churches, they continue to participate in this Mass on Zoom for the support and personal interactions they experience. Unlike watching a streaming Mass on YouTube, which is a very passive experience, they prefer the almost live interactive encounters on a Zoom platform where they can see one another and hear different people talking and singing.

The uncertainty continues with the various COVID-19 variants,[6] but this is not an unprecedented situation. We will overcome the COVID-19 pandemic just as the world emerged from the pandemic of 1918. Furthermore, we have seen that during this period of change, the human person, individually and as a society, has managed to walk through this sudden change and pick up valuable lessons for life.

St. Ignatius of Loyola went through a similar period of uncertainty and change five hundred years ago. The transition from the Middle Ages to the Renaissance, to the Scientific Age, and subsequently the Enlightenment, offers us many ways of not only "hanging on" during these difficult times but also making the best use of and fully flourishing during the times that we are in.

Ignatius's own experience of living with uncertainty and striving to just hang on was during his time in the hospital where he was recovering from a broken leg due to a hit from a cannonball.[7] To back up a little, we see the young Íñigo, in 1521, at the duke's court in Pamplona, Navarre, which was part of the kingdom of Castile. When war broke out against France, Íñigo was asked to lead one section of the army while the other was led by Martín García Óñez. Due to a number of circumstances, Martín got angry and rode off with his troops. Íñigo decided to continue the fight with a handful of volunteers, even though the French army had over twelve thousand men and heavy artillery. Ignatius himself narrates the following in the third person:

> He was in a fortress which the French were attacking and although the others were of the opinion that they should surrender on terms of having their lives spared, as they clearly saw there was no possibility of a defense, he gave so many reasons to the governor that he persuaded him to carry on the defense against the

judgment of the officers, who found some strength in his spirit and courage. On the day on which they expected the attack to take place, he made his confession to one of his companions in arms.[8]

Despite a spirited defense, the castle wall was breached. Ignatius got ready to attack with a sword, but at that very moment, "a cannonball struck him in the leg, crushing his bones and because it passed between his legs, it also seriously wounded the other."[9]

During his recovery in the hospital, Ignatius asked for books on chivalry and gallantry. However, the only two books in that place were *The Life of Jesus* by Carthusian Ludolph of Saxony and one on the lives of the saints, commonly called *The Flos Sanctorum* by Jacobus de Voragine.[10] While reading these books, amid the uncertainty of his future, the question that arose in his mind was, "If Francis of Assisi and the other saints could do so much, what was stopping him?" This moment of conversion could truly be described as the real cannonball moment. When we are placed in times of rapid uncertainty and change, instead of mourning the lack of control that we have over our lives, we could take these times as an opportunity to revisit our lives and the path that we are on. Do we need to reroute our GPS maps? Or with the additional time on our hands, could we take up an old hobby of ours or learn a new skill? Our underlying attitude should be one of optimism and looking toward the future with hope just as young Íñigo did. This enthusiasm and living in the faith need not be pulled out of thin air. Instead, we just look back on our preceding years and see how we have been taken care of and have successfully navigated dangerous waters in our past.

Once his conversion took place, Íñigo began to slowly learn to listen to the gentle promptings of the Holy Spirit within him. What should be the path that he would take? What should be his mission? It is important to realize the struggles that he went through and even the false starts. At that early stage, there was

Uncertainty, Rapid Change, and Ignatius

not even a whisper of a thought of founding the Society of Jesus. At that time, he was thinking of being of service to humanity through God as an individual. His first desire was to visit Jerusalem. Unfortunately, however, he could not get onto the ship that year. Instead, he decided to go to Rome and offer himself in service to the pope. On his way to Rome, he had a deeply spiritual experience at the Chapel of Montmartre dedicated to the Blessed Mother Mary. He heard the mother of Jesus telling her son to take Ignatius as his loyal servant. Later, another spiritual experience took place on the banks of the Cardoner River. All these different spiritual experiences helped him to later write his seminal work, the *Spiritual Exercises*.[11] So, the first setback he experienced in not being able to go to Jerusalem turned out to be a preparation time for him to become a future leader. In Rome, he did some social work for the poor. He would have loved to have carried on working at the grassroots level, but the desire to become a priest was strong. Realizing that he would need an academic background to do so, he soon found himself in school as a much older student in a classroom filled with kids. He eventually attended university, and there he met other young men with whom he would share his spiritual experiences. The idea of getting a couple of companions to accompany him on his mission began to emerge, and a while later, he approached the pope with his intention to form a religious order. But there were many stumbling blocks on this path.[12]

We can draw a couple of lessons from this section of Ignatius's life. First, the time between the seed of an idea being planted in our head and its coming to fruition may be much longer than planned. Therefore, second, we must learn to build our patience muscle. Third, we need a lot of humility on the pathway to achieving our goal. For Ignatius, it meant facing the embarrassment of sitting in a classroom with young boys who would surely have teased him on occasion. Fourth, we realize that the pathway from point A to point B is never an easy, straight line, but the curves and detours have their own role to play. They need not be irritations along the journey, but in fact, they may be very valuable additions.

Uncertainty was not only a personal experience of Ignatius. There was the beginning of the movement out of the so-called Dark Ages to the Scientific Revolution, which became the basis of the later Age of Enlightenment. The Enlightenment applied the principles of logic and reason, on which science based itself, to society, but this would not have been possible without the Renaissance, a cultural and intellectual period that had its highest moments during the fifteenth and sixteenth centuries. There was excitement about classical philosophy, mathematics, and the natural sciences. The church was under attack, and Scholasticism was being abandoned.[13] Thus, a lot of change occurred during the period of Ignatius's life and the formation of the Society of Jesus. As we cope with this pandemic, some of these lessons can hold us in good stead, or for that matter, whenever we are facing uncertainty. We need to hold on to the hope that eventually all the delays, the breaks, and the sudden interruptions will work together to provide a beautiful work of art.

During his convalescence, when he was alone contemplating his future and without the distraction of everyday life, Ignatius began to notice what he would call "movements" taking place within himself. During this quiet time, he became aware of distinctive emotions, but it is said that "he paid no attention to this, nor did he stop to weigh the difference until one day his eyes were opened a little and he began to wonder at the difference and to reflect on it, learning from experience that one kind of thoughts left him sad and the others cheerful. Thus, step by step, he came to recognize the difference between the two spirits that moved him, one being from the evil spirit, the other being from God."[14]

From a modern psychological perspective, we could consider this as voices coming from our brighter side and our darker

Uncertainty, Rapid Change, and Ignatius

nature. From a biological perspective, we could probably identify the darker voice emerging from the evolutionary trait of self-preservation as opposed to the call to move toward our higher nature. The evolutionary trait of self-preservation is codified in what we today call the ego. All that the ego desires is to preserve the individual.[15] This is manifested in the constant recollection of things that have hurt the ego/body. They could be physical or emotional—a taunt/insult expressed through a comment that is meant to degrade the individual. The body/brain deliberately chooses not to forget this harm done to the ego and, therefore, we notice the tendency of the brain to cling on to negative memories in spite of our willingness to move beyond that incident. It is just the nature of the mind to protect the body. On the other hand, if we are to grow to our full potential and maximum human flourishing, we need to heed the call of our higher selves/higher power to move beyond the minimum level of mere self-preservation.

To understand this further, let us look at an overview of a typical movie where a person is shown as a hero (or that's what we think based on the shared commonalities of the values), and the antagonist who shares a different approach than the hero. The scene with the antagonist is that somehow the person's ego is hurt due to our hero, which leads to conflicts and issues. Moreover, the antagonist is so attached to those hurtful moments that the moral system is shattered, and the antihero nature starts manifesting. However, the hero is always shown to have won the fight for values on moral grounds. Such a generalized plot tends to give viewers hope and a sense of responsibility to keep moving forward.

In the next few chapters, we will explain in detail how insights from St. Ignatius can guide us through these times of change and how Ignatian spirituality can help us navigate uncertain times.

2
HEALTH AND HEALING

HEALTH COMES FROM the Latin word *holos*, which means "wholeness." Therefore, a person who enjoys good health is *whole*, with complete well-being of mind, body, and spirit. Modern medicine has advanced the care of the **body** to a great degree where we now have full organ transplants as well as multiple organ transplants like a joint heart and lung transplant.[1] Stem cell treatments tackle the core cellular organization to heal the body. Mapping the genome structure also gives us clues as to whether there is a probability of facing Alzheimer's or dementia after a certain age.[2] It is important to note that the results from DNA testing are merely markers. There are many other factors that will determine, after the age of sixty-five, if one does contract the illness that the marker indicates. These markers may prompt us to make healthy lifestyle changes such as a balanced diet and regular exercise, but feeding the body with unnecessary drugs as a preventive measure for a possible future disease should be entertained with utmost caution.

With regards to the **mind** or specifically to the biological brain, we can maintain that we have made some progress, but this is also up for debate. The current model of psychiatry is based on the premise that all illnesses can be cured by the right type of chemical drug.[3] While certain drugs may be of help up to a point for some very limited cases, the profusion of prescriptive drugs dispensed to millions of people across the world is a cause for alarm. Unlike the biomedical model that insists on double-blind studies, replicability of data, and a meta-analysis of a longitudinal study, most psychiatrists would agree that the field of psychiatry may only be touching upon the surface concerning well-documented proof. We still appear to be in the era of trial and error on some mental illnesses. The long-term side effects of the drugs prescribed for mental health issues still need more studies to understand them better. Additionally, the more important ethical questions of human agency, autonomy, and freedom need further discussion. The illnesses that find a place in the DSM-5 (Diagnostic and Statistical Manual of Mental Disorders) land there because they have been voted upon based on the limited data available.

When we come to the **spirit** aspect of the human, this area is lesser known, to the extent that some even deny the existence of this aspect in a person. What is ironic is that through thousands of years of human history, it was the spirit aspect that was at the center. Thankfully, it is the limitations that we still face even at the height of the advances made by the biomedical sciences that are creating an awareness today that the human person is more than just a mechanical body, and that to truly allow for human flourishing, healing, and holistic health we need to consider all the three aspects of the human person—mind, body, and spirit. All these three aspects are interconnected, and all of us need to understand this. These aspects are not stand-alone, and we will see this as we go ahead.

THE NERVOUS SYSTEMS

Let's begin with neuroscience, the scientific study of the nervous system.[4] It is an interdisciplinary field involving chemistry, biology, and more such disciplines. One aspect of it is studying

UNITING MIND, BODY, SPIRIT

how biological processes relate to behavioral and mental processes. We know that there are three nervous systems. The first one is the *central nervous system*, and the subparts are the brain, the spinal cord, and the retina. Some important parts of the brain associated with emotions are the amygdala, hypothalamus, hippocampus, and limbic cortex consisting of the cingulate gyrus and the parahippocampal gyrus.

Then we have the *peripheral nervous system*, the sympathetic and the parasympathetic subparts; this is the interface between the central nervous system and the environment. The third nervous system is the *enteric nervous system*, more commonly known as the gut. What is not so well-known is the extent to which our thinking affects the gut.

Let me draw the connections. Whenever one is nervous or anxious, it gets reflected in the body. We are familiar with the term "butterflies in the stomach," which refers to the sensation produced in the stomach region before a presentation or an onstage performance. Sometimes, when there is intense anxiety, that might result in stomach pain or constipation. Young children could experience the opposite effect and may have to rush to the restroom. For some people, it might be even more severe like palpitations and difficulty in breathing.

We are all familiar with stress. There are numerous situations in our life when we encounter stress from the time we begin our day, preparing breakfast and getting the kids and ourselves ready for work. Then comes the harassing commute, whether it be securing a seat on the train, or bus, or having to navigate peak-hour traffic jams in our car. The next stage is the workplace, and maybe dealing with a boss or an annoying colleague. Finally, we have the commute back, but it does not end there. Dinner has to be prepared, and the children's homework has to be supervised amid a mountain of other tasks to be accomplished. Then this whole day is repeated once again. This stress does not remain in the mind alone. It expresses itself in the body, albeit differently for each person. For some, it may appear as lower back pain, for others as a stomach upset. When you're tense, it feels so good for someone to massage your shoulders as it at once relieves the tension. For a long time, physicians used the term "psychosomatic illnesses" and would say, "It's all in your mind." That is a partial truth. A psychosomatic illness is in the mind, but that doesn't mean it remains only there. It also expresses itself through our bodies. Repeated doses of stress referred to as "chronic stress" can also lead to ulcers in the stomach and other lifestyle diseases.[5]

All of this reveals how the mind affects the body. This happens when the brain is on autopilot. We don't ask for it. It is just a way in which the body functions. Yet there is good news!

We can do something to change this, and the answer comes from recent research that points to the fact that the brain can change. For a very long time, it was believed that after the initial years of childhood, the brain could not be changed, and there was no way to change it later in life. However, more and more evidence began to appear on the horizon that disputed the perceived wisdom. One of the classic experiments that demonstrate this was done on taxi drivers in London.[6] London was chosen because the roads and streets in London are all over the place in a chaotic manner, unlike the carefully structured streets and avenues that run as a grid system in New York, which was rebuilt after the Great Fire of 1835. The brains of the London taxi drivers who participated in the research were found to have a thicker hippocampus, which is the part of the brain responsible for spatial navigation, learning, and memory. The hippocampus is also called the Global Positioning System (GPS) of the brain. Because the roads in London were complicated, the drivers had to work extra hard to figure out directions and routes to take people from one place to the other. This frequent and ongoing use of the hippocampus led to greater neuronal connections being formed that resulted in the thickening of the hippocampus. From this, we see that the repetition of a particular action causes changes in the brain. Thus, any or all actions done repeatedly actually rewire the brain. Knowing this helps work out strategies to detach the brain from the autopilot mode. Let us now look at one way to do this.

MEDITATION

Meditation can be a powerful tool. Science has some amount of research (albeit nascent) on the benefits of meditation. People doing meditation experience a sense of lightness, the sensation of being one with the world, and a feeling of unity within themselves. At the psychological level, there is a heightened awareness of the sensory field, including a different way of perceiving the relationship between thoughts, feelings, and experience of self. At the physiological level, meditation calms the sensitive vagus nerve, which is responsible for detecting tension in organs associated with stress. Thus, it shuts down the physiological mechanism that causes inflammation due to stress. It alleviates our physiological reaction to stress.[7]

There are various types of meditation. Some work better for one personality type, while others suit different personality types. Even one person on some days might be drawn to one type of meditation and on other days to a different type. That is the beauty of having an array of meditation options at our disposal. The various types of meditation can be broadly categorized under two main headings: concentration and awareness.[8] We will examine awareness methods of meditation in chapter 5 while focusing here on meditation using concentration.

Concentrative techniques use an object for focusing the mind. This could be a picture of God or a beautiful scene from nature. The object could be a lit fireplace or even a simple candle. If we are outdoors, the object could be a palm tree at a distance. Moving beyond the visual, the object could be auditory. In a second method of concentrative meditation, we close our eyes

Health and Healing

and listen to the sounds around us. We begin with the sounds that are closer to us or the loudest. Then we start moving our mental awareness in ever-widening concentric circles around us. After repeating this several times, we will notice that we can pick up sounds in the distance that initially we were not able to hear. An analogy can be drawn to listening to a rich, complicated symphony of Beethoven. Every time we listen to the Ninth Symphony, for example, we hear things that we had possibly missed earlier on. This could be a triplet around a melody note or a wind instrument coming in as an echo to what the pianist is playing. The overall effect in both visual and sound meditation[9] is getting out of the chatter of the mind and focusing on any one thing that ultimately brings us to a place of calm.

The third method of concentrative meditation is focusing on our breathing. From the yoga tradition, we have "pranayama," from the Buddhist tradition we have "vipassana," and within the Christian tradition, I have developed the Holy Spirit Rosary. The main principles involve drawing our awareness to our breathing, as we breathe in and as we breathe out. It sometimes helps to narrow our focus of attention to the area around the nostrils, constantly being aware that we are breathing in and breathing out. There is no need to attempt to change or deepen our breathing. During the meditation, simply focus on your breathing just as it is. However, at the start of the breathing meditation, or for that matter any type of meditation, it is helpful to take three or four deep breaths—breathing in slowly and breathing out all our stresses, worries, and anxieties that we may hold at the time of starting the meditation. When breathing out, it is as if we were letting out a huge sigh of relief, letting go of the stresses of the day. After three or four breaths, we allow our body to return to its normal breath pace. We keep our focus on breathing in and breathing out.

All meditative techniques aim at reducing the chatter of the mind.[10] We may have heard the phrase "monkey mind" or the statement, "Your mind is like a monkey on a hot tin roof with firecrackers tied to its tail." With this imagery in mind, we can truly imagine our minds jumping from one thought to the other like that monkey on a hot tin roof. Another oft-repeated sentence from Buddhist literature is, "The mind is like a thousand elephants in a jungle fleeing from a forest fire." The outcome of meditation is a calming of the mind, a sense of stillness, and a feeling of peace.

A MEDITATION EXERCISE

Figure 1
Please scan this QR code to access the Guided Breath Meditation.

I invite you to join me in a brief meditation experience.

1. First, choose a posture with your back erect, either sitting on a chair or cross-legged on the floor if you are comfortable with that. You need not keep the back stiffly erect. It should be straight and yet relaxed.
2. Keep your hands on your lap, palms facing upward, open in a gesture of surrender. Or the fingertips of both hands touching each other, almost similar to the hands in prayer position, but without the palms touching each other.

Health and Healing

3. Then close your eyes gently. This helps with concentration. Some people find concentration better with their eyes slightly open, looking at the ground in front of them in a sort of blurred vision.
4. Then begin by taking three or four deep breaths. Breathe in and then out as if you were sighing, letting go of all your tensions, feeling your shoulders relaxing as your body lets go.
5. After a couple of deep breaths, let your breathing return to its normal pace without trying to control any part of it.
6. Now, focus your attention on your breathing. I am breathing in. I am breathing out. I am breathing in. I am breathing out. Focus your attention on your normal breathing. I am breathing in. I am breathing out.
7. Some people find it helpful to narrow the focus of attention to the area around the nostrils rather than the stomach or diaphragm. This may help to increase your concentration.
8. Carry on focusing on your breathing in the area around the nostrils.
9. Feel your whole body already relaxing, letting go. It also helps to keep your face in a gentle smile, more like the beginning of a smile. At no point should the body be tensed up. Totally relaxed, totally calm. If distracting thoughts come into your mind—as they will—gently say, "Thank you for reminding me about that. I will attend to you later," and return to focusing on your breathing.
10. Know that it is the nature of the mind to resist focusing on just one thing. The mind loves to jump about from one thought to the other. So, don't get

UNITING MIND, BODY, SPIRIT

upset if you find your mind wandering. As soon as you realize it has wandered, gently bring it back to focusing on your breathing.

11. Some people find it helpful to breathe in groups of ten, like when saying the Rosary or counting on beads. Small victories offer an impetus to keep going. If you would like to try that, you can do so now.
12. For those used to saying the Rosary, one could add an Our Father at the start and then on the ten breaths, you could say "Come Holy Spirit," and as you breathe out, "I surrender all." And at the end, say the Glory Be. This is, in essence, the Holy Spirit Rosary.
13. The main aim is to keep returning to your breathing. Success in meditation is not how long you were able to breathe without being distracted, but how soon you became aware of distraction and returned to the breathing. As you get more familiar with meditation, you will begin to bring your attention back quicker if your mind does wander off.
14. We will be ending this meditation session in one minute, so concentrate fully once again on your breathing.
15. Now slowly return back into consciousness, into awareness of where you are in the room, and as and when you are ready, you can slowly get up. Take your time. When you are ready, that is the correct time.

ASKING FOR GRACE

An important aspect of meditation that Ignatius insisted upon is the "ask." In his language, ask for the grace you're seeking. In your mind, you should be clear about the outcome that

Health and Healing

you're seeking; what is it that you want to achieve? You will gain this clarity upon completing the step of Discernment of Spirits, as developed in the next chapter. St. Ignatius would say that we have to ask for the grace we seek before going to bed at night, as soon as we get up in the morning, and a couple of times during the day. It leads us to the next aspect of St. Ignatius's writing, namely, the power of repetition.

While repetition is a significant feature when asking for a desired outcome, it is also important when seeking to bring about behavior change. Most of us can recollect how we were made to write and rewrite the alphabet till we mastered it. We were asked to memorize the multiplication table till our lips turned blue. Learning a new language also calls for writing, revising, and repetition. For this reason, I like to refer to St. Ignatius as a neuroscientist before his time. From neuroscience, we see how any experience that is repeated consciously and continuously results in a thickening of a neuronal pathway that then leads to that behavior becoming your habit. Hence, any new behavior that we seek to develop, or any behavioral change that we envisage, requires a replication of that new way of acting. If we are seeking to be more compassionate, we begin by seeking out opportunities to exercise compassion in our day-to-day living, whether it be at the workplace, in our neighborhood, or our homes. Once compassion is practiced over and over, the brain goes on autopilot, and compassion becomes our natural way of being. Keep asking yourself the question, "What do I practice every day?" because that which you practice will become perfect in you. If you practice negative thinking, you will become perfect in being critical. If you practice compassion, you will become a compassionate being.

Let us see how this works concerning healing and health. For example, if I want to lose weight, I first have to make the ask to my body. I place this intention before my higher power and keep the image of myself at my desired weight in mind. It also

UNITING MIND, BODY, SPIRIT

helps to write it on a post-it and stick this around my room. I then write down the long-term and short-term steps required to reach this goal. I practice food behaviors that will help me stay away from eating in between meals, snacking, grazing, or just throwing candy into my mouth because it is freely available in the office lounge. During mealtimes, I decide beforehand how much to eat and what to eat. When these behaviors become part of a daily regime, they become a habit. One would be surprised to note that Ignatius also writes about moderation in food and food behavior.

Let us now apply some of these principles to the constant negative thoughts in our minds. The mind loves to dwell in the past or think about the future.[11] This may conjure feelings of regret, the guilt of things done or left undone in the past. This also brings up feelings of anxiety and worry about the future. We may feel guilty because of our friends and family who have died due to COVID-19. At the same time, the uncertainty of the future brings about stress and the resultant feelings of doubt, nervousness, and worry. How do we address this constant negativity playing out in the theater of our minds? We will be answering this question ahead.

3

DECISION-MAKING
A Leap of Faith?

DURING TIMES OF stability, it is perhaps easy to make decisions as we have most of the influential factors needed at our fingertips. Furthermore, we also have some surety that the parameters we are taking into consideration will not change suddenly. On the other hand, during times of uncertainty, the variables that we have to factor into our decision-making are not all there. Even among the ones that are at our disposal, we are unsure about the time frame of validity for these variables. Thus, decision-making will seem very hard. It might seem contrary, but it is imperative that during times of rapid change we continue to take the risk of making decisions. Emotions of anxiety, nervousness, and apprehension will be a part of this process.

DISCERNMENT OF SPIRITS

Ignatius recognized the conflicting chatter that goes on in our minds, especially how difficult it is to decide on something. Do we take the road on our left or the road on our right? At times, the mind throws up many reasons to choose the road on the left. At other times, we seem to have an equal number of reasons to choose the road on the right. This can get very confusing and can even result in paralysis of action. Ignatius went through this himself and from his experience produced the seminal work on "Discernment of Spirits." We need to acknowledge our confusing thoughts and yet decide to move forward. It is absolutely normal to not want to act sometimes. Just accept that fact and look for a better path in order to avoid a paralysis of action.

Ignatius has cautioned us not to make life-changing decisions during times of personal emotional upheaval. He advises us to maintain the status quo, maintain our connection with God, and await the time when your mind and heart have reached a peaceful state to make the decision. This should not be confused with what we have said earlier. Life has to go on! During difficult times, we may move forward only in inches and not in leaps and bounds, but move forward we must.

At the very start, we need to be aware that for Ignatius the primary aim of the *Spiritual Exercises*, including that of the "Discernment of Spirits," is to bring us into union and communion with God. For a wider audience, we can frame it as the goal and purpose of our lives. Or as Paul Coutinho, a scholar on Ignatian spirituality, puts it, "What do you want on your tombstone?" Discernment has to become a way of life for us. Whenever we are making decisions, we need to ask ourselves, "Is this helping me to reach the goal of my life?" Coutinho has divided the process of Discernment of Spirit into three instances.[1] First is the situation when we are faced with tremendous clarity and have no doubt about which option we should follow. Second, we make a decision, listening to how we feel within us, often referred to as picking up the movements within you. Ignatius uses the words *consolations* and *desolations*. Third, we put down the pros and cons, then we try to pick up consolations and desolations, and then we attempt to see which decision will help us reach our ultimate goal. I will spell out for you the steps in detail.

Decision-Making

One of the first things that we do when deciding between two "goods" is to take a sheet of paper and put down in writing the choices we have. Then, on each of the sheets we make two columns where we list down positives and negatives of each. The process of getting these thoughts out of our minds and putting them on paper already takes us to a greater degree of clarity. After having "put the thoughts on paper," read them two or three times and then let them sit in the recesses of your mind. Ask your higher power to enlighten you when you next take up the discernment process. After a day or two, you can revisit the two pages. You will now find that some of the reasons that you put down earlier are not so important, and some other reasons that may have surfaced need to be put down. Now look at this revised list on both sides and then move from your mind to the heart.

What is your heart telling you? You may notice that sometimes even if the number of positive points for option A are much more than those for option B, your heart may be drawn to option B. Make a note of this. After this, spend another day or two in prayer and reflection asking your higher power to illuminate both your mind and your heart and to help you come to a decision. Keep asking yourself which of the two options is more closely aligned with the ultimate goal of your life. Depending on the time available to you, you may want to set a date on which you make a final decision. Setting a date prevents you from getting into an endless cycle of oscillating between the two options. Know that on the day you do decide, you may not get the instant comfort of certainty, nor will you experience a sense of confirmation. But you are taking that decision after a time of deep thought, reflection, and prayer. Your decision will be a leap of faith. Even after having made the decision, it is the nature of the mind to slam you between the two options. Don't give in to the temptation of revisiting your decision. Neither is this a time for rethinking, regrets, or guilt.

In most cases, the confirmation of your decision will come days, weeks, or months after you have made that decision. Until then, you can rest in the satisfaction of knowing that you have avoided procrastination and have made the decision at that moment in time based on the evidence that you had before you.

St. Ignatius uses the language of the good spirit and the evil spirit. We need not be drawn into the discussion of whether that is appropriate for our times. However, it is important to remember that this process of discernment that Ignatius gave us is for the times when we are choosing between two goods. It cannot be used when deciding whether you punch your neighbor in the face or write him a polite letter explaining why you are upset with him.

USING THE PROCESS

Remember that the process involves moving from the brain to the heart via the spirit. If we were to put down a sequence for decision-making using St. Ignatius's "Discernment of Spirits," the steps would be as follows:

1. Begin with a prayer asking for the guidance of God through the wisdom of the Holy Spirit.
2. Logically put down the points for and against a particular course of action.
3. Then put down the pros and cons of the alternate course of action.
4. Move these various ideas around in your brain for a certain amount of time, and feel free to add new points or subtract some of the points you have put down if they no longer add to the discussion.
5. Once again invoke the blessings of God and ask for further guidance as you move on from the brain to the heart.

Decision-Making

6. Quiet yourself, spend time in meditation, and then be prepared to listen to what the heart has to say. Another way to discern is to see which of the options are eliciting a greater energy from within. Sometimes it may happen that even though option A may have more points in its favor, logically speaking, the heart may be directing you to option B.
7. Repeat step 6 after a day or two and see if you are getting a similar affirmation or if something has changed.
8. Make the final decision even though you may not have 100 percent certainty or receive a clear confirmation with regards to the path that you have chosen. Be assured that the confirmation will come later after you make the choice through a "leap of faith."

It is important to note that when one attempts to make a decision only using the brain/logical mind, one gets slammed back and forth between opposite walls. The good thing about the mind is that it allows us to see various angles of the issue at hand, but it is not very helpful in giving us a clear answer as to the path that we have to take. There is, of course, the option of tossing a coin. St. Ignatius did this in the early stage of his spiritual journey as he narrates in his autobiography with regard to the incident of the Moor. On his journey to the shrine of Montserrat, a Moor caught up with him, and they began talking. However, a while later, they disagreed on one issue. Noticing that Ignatius was getting agitated, the Moor moved on ahead and passed out of sight. Pondering on what had just happened—and feeling that he had not done his duty—there arose within Ignatius a desire to seek out the Moor and do him harm.

He had a long struggle over this desire and at the end remained in doubt...at last, tired of examining what would be best to do and unable to reach a fixed conclusion, he decided to drop the reins and let his mule go uncontrolled to the point where the roads divided. If the animal took the road to the town indicated, he would seek out the Moor and poniard him; if it kept to the high road, avoiding the town, he would let him be...though the town stood little more than 30–40 paces away, and the road to it was very broad and good, it pleased God that the mule kept to the *Camino Real* and avoided the road to the town.[2]

As you can see, Ignatius also did a version of tossing the coin. But this method is best kept for small, inconsequential decisions.

Returning to the process of discernment, after one has spent time thinking of the various options, one has to leave the mind, so to speak, and descend into the realm of the metaphorical heart to listen to the still, small voice. It will slowly emerge from deep within once we have been able to silence the chatter of the mind. In other words, listen to the wisdom of the body when the mind is quiet.

A question could be asked, "Since we know that the heart makes a favorable decision for us, can we bypass the mind and listen only to the heart?" Very often, we hear the phrase, "Sheela thinks with her heart only." Or "Tom's heart has been captured by Meena." Or "Anil has *fallen* in love." All of these refer to the use of the heart or a decision that has been taken based on our emotions alone. One could say that in certain exceptional cases one could go with the decision of the metaphorical heart alone. Once in a blue moon, the heart emphatically speaks to us regarding a path to be taken. In such rare cases, one feels an absolute certainty and clarity about the way forward, not even needing any process to be followed. "I clearly know what I have to do!" But most of the time, and more importantly when it involves a long-term decision or a life decision, it would be wiser to bring in the mind. Thus, for most decisions it is necessary to make use of both the mind and the heart as described in the process above.

When we make a decision, we will not know if it is good or bad immediately since the confirmation for the decision comes later. Another question can arise in our mind, "How can I still go ahead?" First of all, it is important to remember that the whole decision-making process outlined above is used when we are choosing between two good options. One would hope that one does not use this process for choosing between a good and an evil outcome. In some cases where the confirmation comes during the process of discernment, it makes it easier to then act on the decision. But as rightly pointed out, in most cases one has to take a leap of faith. The confirmation will follow. Since this process is used to decide between two good alternatives, once the decision is made, it is necessary to invest all your energy into making that decision work. When we come to the table bringing with us all of the passion that we possess, life /universe / God provides help /guidance /insights to keep our project moving forward. In the end, when we look back on our life's journey, we will have the satisfaction of seeing that somehow all of the choices that we made have come together. It makes up the beautiful life that we have led; not despite all its ups and downs, but poignantly because of all its ups and downs.

In other words, because we have spent a considerable amount of time going through the discernment process, we can trust the process and our final instinct. We can have confidence in ourselves that the viable option we are going to choose will turn out to be the best one at this point in time. Quite often we have in our minds the notion that there is a detailed architectural plan for our lives embedded somewhere in the ether. Our task is to discover this map carved out in stone. A better way of understanding this is that there is possibly a blueprint, a general outline, based on our genetic make-up and our environmental influences. As we journey through life based on our choices, this blueprint evolves into a detailed line drawing. A further aspect of this process is that as we make decisions, and work to put them into practice and experience success, our confidence level in our own decision-making capabilities keeps on rising. As we progress along this path, we go through less and less of our former experience of being slammed between the opposite walls of our options.

AN EXAMPLE OF DISCERNMENT

The first time I was introduced to the process of "Discernments of Spirits" was when I began to sense within me the call to the Society of Jesus. This happened about six months before the end of the academic year in the midst of all of the plans that I was already considering after graduation. My father was keen that I do a management course, as an MBA would help in a mini business venture that he was contemplating starting by himself, after retiring from his job. This was at the same time I was due to graduate with a bachelor's degree. I was also involved in a major theatrical production then, both in singing and choreography, as well as lending my voice for jingles. As a result, whenever that still, small voice would surface from within inviting me to consider a life of service as a Jesuit, I kept drowning it out by keeping busy and considering other options, hoping it would go away. Unfortunately, that did not work, so I approached the Jesuit counselor on campus hoping to hear from him that this voice was only in my imagination and that I needed to carry on with my life. Instead, he invited me to walk through the discernment process. I dutifully filled in the plus and minus columns and would take it to prayer. Still, I did not get a clear answer. When I shared the news with my parents, my mother—though initially opposed—later became supportive of the idea. My father, on the other hand, was vehemently opposed to the idea on the grounds

Decision-Making

of my being the only son and the eldest child. As he would say, "If I had a second boy, I would have willingly let you go. The family name needs to carry on. Furthermore, if your vocation is to serve, you can do that even as a married man." Hence, I was torn between the valid arguments of my father, the exciting life the world had to offer me, and that small voice in my imagination. So, I kept pleading with God to give me a clear sign if it was really God behind that quiet voice within me inviting me to become a priest.

Finally, when I completed my graduation, I was still being tossed between the two options of joining or not joining religious life. In the meantime, without my knowledge, my father went to the Provincial of the Society of Jesus and had a long argument about why he should refuse my admission to the Society. The provincial then suggested to me at a later meeting that I do my master's in chemistry since this would give enough time for my father to adjust to the new situation. The thought that occurred to me was, "Would the desire and the call to join still be there after two years?" Anyway, I didn't have much say in the situation, and I was still conflicted within myself. So, I immersed myself in my graduate studies in inorganic chemistry, while at the same time working in Mumbai theater. As the two years of study drew to a close, I visited the novitiate, the house of formation in Nashik. Staying among the Jesuit novices there and partaking in their daily routine for three days, I felt a sense of calm and a feeling that I should at least give this way of life a trial even if I didn't get a clear confirmation.

One of the reasons that my father had given me against joining the Jesuits was that my bachelor's degree was not something that I could fall back upon should I decide later that religious life was not really my path. Now, on the verge of completing my master's degree, I went once again to him to seek his blessings to join the Jesuits. His reply was, "You know, son, today even an MSc degree may not fetch you a good job. You do your PhD and

UNITING MIND, BODY, SPIRIT

I will gladly give you my blessings." By this time, I was an adult, twenty-two years of age, and I decided to make a leap of faith and join the Society of Jesus. The actual confirmation of my decision to join came three months later after I was already in the novitiate. I had just received my master's results and had achieved a first class. These results were sent to me by my father along with a huge cake for all of the novices. He just wrote two words on a piece of paper, "Congratulations! —Daddy." For me, these two words meant a lot because this was the first time he had communicated with me since I had left home. In fact, a month before I joined the novitiate, he had gone to our second home in Goa, our hometown, and I had to leave without his blessings. On the day I received this note from him, I suddenly experienced the confirmation of my decision to join the Society. The cascade of positive events and my father's blessings turned out to be the confirmation I needed. I began to feel a deep sense of peace.

4

BRAIN AND BEHAVIOR CHANGE

LET US BEGIN with a narrative, a story that spreads over the whole world. We will begin with California in the United States and fly across the world to India.

This is the story of Wayne (the name is changed). He was your typical skateboarder in California, who started out simply by going to the skate park. He could see people performing all sorts of stunts, and he wanted to fit in. So, he stepped into the park. Eventually, the skaters showed him all their tricks, and he learned everything that he needed to know. But he still yearned for something more. Wayne soon moved to the beaches and took up surfboarding, which gave him far more thrills because of the danger involved. He became very good at surfboarding as well. But then he was looking for a much higher kick. A lot of surfboarders would meet after their time on the waves to drink a beer and to chill. Wayne began to join them. From beer, they gradually went on to mild drugs. But they were always in search of the next big high. And so, within no time they moved on to truly addictive drugs: heroin and cocaine. Today, Wayne can share his experience of how he got addicted to chemical drugs, which form an important type of substance addiction (along with, for example, alcohol and nicotine).

There are medicinal drugs, which doctors prescribe to make some therapeutic changes, but these same drugs could lead to addiction in the same manner as recreational drugs like marijuana and the more addictive heroin and cocaine.[1] When we speak of a chemical imbalance, we are referring to a balance that can be restored by seeking a remedy in therapeutic chemicals, namely, medicinal drugs. Outside medical establishments a person may seek to alter his/her chemical responses in some way through chemicals that are nothing but addictive drugs. These may be legal or illegal to consume. Such drugs do many of the same things as naturally occurring neurotransmitters—the body's chemical messengers. Drugs can imitate neurotransmitters or modify what they do, even block neurotransmitter action. They can have deep, lasting, and profound effects on the brain.[2] A very common question is, "How do I know that I am addicted to something?" There are things that we like, things that we may want, and things that our bodies may need. But if we are craving a particular substance regularly and can't seem to stop, we may consider ourselves addicted.

HOW DO DRUGS WORK?

Cognitive enhancers are taken to improve mental functions. These mind-altering drugs change a neuron's ability to release transmitters and check how a neuron receives them. So, a chemical can activate the receptor, or it can bind to the receptor and not activate it, preventing other chemicals from getting in.[3] In most cases, drugs work on signaling pathways connected to biochemical signaling inside neurons.

Some may ask, "How did you get to neuroscience from your initial specialization in chemistry?" My reply is that neuroscience is nothing but chemistry of the brain. These chemicals are synthesized biogenic amines, serotonin, adrenaline (which is the word used outside the United States in place of epinephrine), and histamine. These biogenic amines have important roles in regulating mood, learning, movement, and basic physiological responses.[4] They regulate personality and the way one comes across to another. We now come to a neurotransmitter whose name is well-known even among laypeople—dopamine. Dopamine is especially important in executive function, in regulating movements. When it reduces in supply, a disease like Parkinson's can occur. Also, when uptake blockers affect dopamine function, it leads to "addiction."[5] The drugs, including Prozac, LSD (lysergic acid diethylamide), MDMA (ecstasy), amphetamines, antihistamines, and cocaine cause the dopamine, which seems to convey a sense of reward, to linger in the synapse and the neural tissue. Ritalin, which increases the amount of dopamine, is used for attention deficit hyperactivity disorder (ADHD) and can also lead to addiction.

Most of us cannot do without a cup of coffee in the morning and maybe a cup of tea in the afternoon, but the effect of mild drugs like caffeine can be reversed if we so desire. One day, you decide that you are going to go off caffeine; it is relatively easy to stop the withdrawal symptoms from coffee and tea. But when it comes to hard drugs, it is anything but easy as such drugs are actually making physical changes in your brain.

How do these changes come about? Nicotine is another drug that binds to receptors for acetylcholine, and they can alter the sensitivity of neurons and long-term learning mechanisms. Besides being addictive and habit-forming, nicotine receptor activation can enhance brain function. Sometimes, when you smoke a cigarette, initially you are all relaxed and you can do a lot of good work, but down the line you have decreased efficiency. Some drugs that reduce the symptoms of Alzheimer's disease enhance function by acting on nicotinic acetylcholine receptors. The main reward center of the brain is the nucleus accumbens, a region in the forebrain. It modulates the emotional strength of the signals originating in the hippocampus.

UNITING MIND, BODY, SPIRIT

Let's take social media as another example. What do you feel when you get a like on your Facebook posts? What are your emotions when someone gives you positive comments on a video you just posted on YouTube? When you receive a large number of views? When the number of subscribers on your channel increases? These same questions can be asked with regards to your X (Twitter) handle, Instagram, Snapchat, or any of the other social media platforms that you use. The general answer to the above questions is that one feels good, affirmed, excited, and motivated. The reward centers in the brain get activated. Because we like this momentary "high," we go out in search of more. It has been found that over 50 percent of the time, people check their phones even though there is no ring or alert.[6] Why do we do that? Because the pleasure centers of the brain are activated.

The hippocampus, while not one of the reward centers of the brain, is linked to the nucleus accumbens and can be considered, indirectly, to be a reward center.[7] Memory and learning take place in the hippocampus. When the nucleus accumbens is activated due to something pleasurable, that instantaneous thrill becomes a memory and over time gets consolidated. The amygdala is the seat of emotions in the brain. The feel-good factor that we experience when we get a like or multiple views for our post is located here. All of these parts of the brain—the nucleus accumbens, the amygdala, and indirectly the hippocampus—are considered to jointly make up the reward centers of the brain. These same centers are the ones that are activated for people addicted to alcohol, drugs, and food; and similarly, for those with nonsubstance or behavioral addiction.

BEHAVIORAL ADDICTIONS

We started with Wayne from California, and we now move to Raj from Delhi. Raj is a tech guy and is addicted to his phone.

Brain and Behavior Change

He constantly checks his WhatsApp, Instagram, and other social media accounts and gets worried if his friends don't like his posts. He is not just addicted to his phone but has a profound addiction to his virtual social circle. He even gets up a few times at night to check his phone to see if he has any calls, a message, a new like, or a new post. This has become so routine for him that, when someone in his house pointed out that this behavior was strange, his immediate reaction was to go on the defensive. It was only much later while he was in treatment that he began to realize that getting up multiple times in the night to check one's phone is a clear sign of being addicted.

From California to Delhi, such situations exist all across the world, whether we are addicted to our phones, our tablets, our devices, or any substance. What, then, is the extent of damage done to our brains by this pharmaceutically enhanced (for example, Ritalin for ADHD, Paxil for shyness), gadget-driven twenty-first century? It is not all negative, surprisingly!

Research has pointed out some positives with regards to the use of gadgets, games, and devices.[8] Users become bright, nimble decision-makers. They can find answers quickly. All of us are a part of the Google clinic, where if we don't know the answer to some question, we refer to Dr. Google and within a fraction of a second, we get our answer. Visual skills improve; the ability to process information gets better.

On the negative side, users become intellectual lightweights. They are unable to concentrate and can easily become distracted. The thirst for instant gratification becomes endemic. There is a lack of deep-thinking skills because they do not allow time for reflection, analysis, or critical thinking. There is a stagnation in technology and even in literature as attention spans shorten. Reading for pleasure enhances thinking and engages the imagination. When we read a book, we have to use our minds to imagine what is going on in it. We picture an array of scenarios. Thus, our brain is being activated. In contrast, when we are looking at our devices, we have all of the visuals at our fingertips; everything is there for us. This somehow hinders creativity and imagination.

Why, then, is nonsubstance addiction a problem? Up to the 1960s, the general belief was that the brain developed in early childhood and after that it was set. The whole concept of IQ, which distinguishes various levels of intelligence, was based on the fact that the brain was fixed. Thus, one could peg a person in a given slot such as genius (scores over 140), superintelligence (scores between 120 and 140), and superior intelligence (scores between 110 and 119). Scores between 80 and 89 were pegged as dullness, and scores under 70 were defined as feeble-mindedness.[9] After the 1960s, more and more research emerged that began to put into question the prevalent understanding that the brain was fixed. So, we began to see that the physical structure of the brain could be changed. New experiences, new learning, can change the structure of the brain.

At birth, every neuron in the cerebral cortex has 2,500 synapses. Later, it goes to 15,000, but after a time, it comes down because of what is called "strengthening and pruning." Just as we need to prune our garden and our trees, our neurons also get pruned, and this is called "synaptic pruning." Neurons that are used frequently develop stronger connections, and those that are rarely, or never, used eventually die. By developing new connections and pruning away weak ones, the brain adapts to the changing environment. You may have heard of the phrase, "Use it or lose it." This applies to the brain. If you learn a new language as an adult, you have to keep at it. As long as you are among those who speak that language, you remember it well, but if you move away from that context, you forget the language as you are not using it that much. Certain skills that we learn when we are children, we don't forget because those have been moved into our long-term memory.

The 2006 study on London taxi drivers mentioned in chapter 2 is an important landmark in understanding that the brain can change even in adult life.[10] To refresh your adult memory, there is a marked difference in London roads as opposed to New York roads. After the Great Fire of the nineteenth century, New York roads were built on a grid system that was symmetrically planned as avenues and streets. Most of the roads in London, however, are built on top of the bullock cart tracks from centuries earlier. There is no system but only turns and twists all over the place. London taxi drivers, hence, have to constantly use the hippocampus in the brain, which is involved in navigation and remembering directions. In other words, the hippocampus can be called the traditional GPS (Global Positioning System) of the body. It is an area of the brain known for spatial navigation. Note that this was before the time of Google Maps, which helps us drive around today.

Researchers examined the brains of these London taxi drivers and found that the hippocampus was much thicker than that of the standard person. So, we see that there is an actual physical change in the brain due to repeated behavior. From this, the conclusion was that daily repeated experiences bring about an actual change in the brain. New experiences cause new synaptic connections to be generated and this results in rewiring of the brain. Therefore, the brain is no longer considered as fixed but is instead described as plastic. This concept is referred to as the neuroplasticity of the brain. More time spent on an activity leads to a rewiring of the brain. Consequently, the long stretches of time spent on smartphones or gaming devices can change the physical shape of the brain. This physical rewiring can also occur in cases of repetitive behaviors leading to addiction. The excess time spent on technology could thus be a cause for concern.

A study was done on eighteen college-age students who satisfied addict criteria, that is, they spent over ten hours a day on internet use.[11] Think for a moment. Is there anyone that you know who would be on the internet for ten hours a day or more, apart from work-related use? When calculating the time, we are referring to all of the devices one may spend time on, such as a smartphone, tablet, laptop, and smart TV. At least, among young audiences, it is very easy to find people who meet the addict criteria. The researchers also selected eighteen healthy controls who spent less than two hours on online games. All were placed into an MRI to undergo two types of brain scans. Specialized scans showed changes in the white matter of the brain in web addicts compared to nonaddicts. There was evidence of disruption in connections to nerve fibers spotlighting brain areas involved in emotions, decision-making, and self-control. The result also suggests that internet addiction disorder (IAD) may also share psychological and neural mechanisms with other types of substance addiction and impulse control. Additionally, white matter abnormalities in the orbitofrontal cortex and other significant brain areas were found not only in substance addiction but also in behavioral addictions such as internet addiction.[12]

Shrinkage could also lead to negative effects such as reduced inhibition of inappropriate behavior and diminished goal orientation in students. Now we see, as we move from substance addiction to nonsubstance addiction, similar types of changes are taking place in the brain. The same areas of the brain are getting activated.

In another research study,[13] twelve experienced web users and twelve digital newcomers used Google while their brains were scanned. The results pointed out a key initial difference between the two groups in an area of the brain called the dorsolateral prefrontal cortex. This area deals with short-term memory and decision-making. The rookies showed hardly any activity, whereas the web veterans were really firing. Six days later, the novices were told to spend an hour a day online, and the two groups' brains were scanned again. This time, in images of both sets of brains, the pattern of blobs representing mental activity was virtually identical. This showed that five hours on the internet for the newcomers had already rewired their brains.

Brain and Behavior Change

What we learn is that even in those online novices there appears to be rewiring of the brain taking place when they graduate to increased amounts of gaming. The brain is very sensitive to any kind of stimulation and from moment to moment, there is a complex cascade of neurochemical electrical consequences to every form of stimulation. If you have repeated stimuli, your neural circuits will be excited. But if you neglect other stimuli, other neural circuits will be weakened.

Our online habits are altering the very structures of our brain. Today, as soon as children cry, what do the parents give them? Not a bottle of milk, but a digital tablet! We are still in the initial stages of all this research, but it points to the fact that repeated experiences alter the brain, even, if not more so, in children. It affects learning and memory. It taxes the parts of the brain that deal with fleeting and temporary matter. Our ability to learn suffers and our understanding remains shallow.

Let me introduce two new terms here: *digital natives* and *digital immigrants*. The former are those who have grown up using digital devices. The latter are those who began to use devices at a much later age. Digital natives repeatedly show a lack of basic human skills like maintaining eye contact or noticing nonverbal cues in a conversation. Social networking sites may be changing people's brains as well as their social life, research suggests.[14] Brain scans show a direct link between the number of Facebook friends people have and the size of certain parts of their brains.[15] The regions (the right superior temporal sulcus, the left middle temporal gyrus, and the right entorhinal cortex) involved have roles in social interaction, memory, and autism. Previous research[16] has shown a link between the volume of grey matter in the amygdala and the size and complexity of real-world social networks. Text messages are dampening human creativity because we are not thinking outside the box. We are constantly tossing about ideas with our friends online. In the past few decades, if you thought of something, you would ruminate over it and let a few days go by, before returning to revise it. But today, as soon as we get an idea, we put it up on X (Twitter) or Facebook, someone else comments on it, someone else jumps on it, and very soon that idea is no longer ours. It has gone into a public space.

Multitasking, the internet's essential modus operandi, is not an efficient way of doing things.[17] We make far more errors, and there's a tendency to do things faster but sloppier. We have spoken about how activities change our brains. Now when we speak of multitasking, it's something that all of us do, but it has been found that the brain does not really multitask. The brain can do only one thing at a time, but we get the impression that it can multitask because it jumps from one thing to another so fast. I am going to segue my way into a related topic and then come back to multitasking with this new information.

One feature of our brain is the existence of the right hemisphere and the left hemisphere. All actions on the right side of our body are controlled by the left hemisphere. The actions on the left side are controlled by the right hemisphere. For pedagogical purposes and convenience, this division of tasks is helpful. But in most cases, both sides of the brain are working all of the time.[18] We are in a right-handed world. Most of us tend to use our right hand for the majority of our daily tasks. Thus, the left side of our brain gets more exercised. Furthermore, our whole educational system focuses on developing logical thinking, linear thinking, and other skills such as verbal communication, planning, math, science, and detail-oriented perception. Logically, then, in order to develop those skills residing in the right side of the brain, we could use our left hand for more and more of our daily tasks. This would enable a greater development of intuition, creativity, emotional balance, writing, art, imagination, and non-verbal communication.

Therefore, those who are left-handed are blessed. Quite a few poets, artists, and musicians are left-handed. Pianists, for example, are taught to play musical scales with both the right hand and left hand from an early age. Most students of the piano realize that they have to spend more time practicing with the left hand to make it as competent as the right hand, but all this extra work on the left hand reaps huge benefits because it helps in developing creativity and perception, much needed skills for advanced musicians. I love to use the example of the boogie to illustrate this. The boogie is a genre of music that has a fairly constant bassline while the treble, which is played by the right hand, does something totally different. This is one example of multitasking that produces beautiful music. As we have seen above, multitasking is a mixed blessing. It does produce some benefits in some cases whereas in others, the benefits might be very little at best and illusionary at worst. We have to be careful that the behavior of multitasking does not become addictive. No longer can we sit quietly and attend to one task at hand. The inherent tendency is to seek out something else to do at the same time. Becoming aware that we may likely be addicted to multitasking is the first step to remedy the situation.

The phenomenon of multitasking is a mixed bag. This aspect is very similar to internet use. The internet's cacophony of stimuli, this crazy quilt of information, has given rise to cursory reading, hurried and distracted thinking, and superficial learning. This contrasts with the Age of the Book, when humans were encouraged to be contemplative and imaginative. However, we have the capacity to pull ourselves back from the mental brink. The brain can correct itself. Technology lures us; our brains become addicted. But we can take back control! It can be done.

I invite you to try this exercise with your friend or sibling. Hand over your phone to them (shutdown mode) for safekeeping for a period of four hours a day. During this time, note down some of your feelings from not having the phone with you. Resist the urge to get back to your phone before the end of the four hours. Most people have found that the first time they do this exercise, they experience a lot of discomfort, anxiety, and the temptation to get the phone back before time. But when this exercise of shutting down the phone and keeping it away from the body for increasing lengths of time is done repeatedly, one begins to find that anxiety is replaced by a feeling of peace. This simple exercise demonstrates that we can pull ourselves back from the edge of the abyss of addiction. We can work to rewire our brains.

Now, I'm going to ask you to do a second exercise. Think of one area of your life that may follow addictive patterns. Maybe it is not drugs, maybe it is not the phone, but maybe you love chocolate. I can't do without my chocolate fix. Maybe you love food or maybe you love something else. Think of any area of your life that you're addicted to; it may not even be considered an addiction. Maybe you don't have a name for it. Is there something in your life that's not going right? Is there something that you'd like to change? Is there something in your life that makes no sense? Do you feel like just giving up? Are there times in your life when you've had enough? Are there times when the clouds seem all black? Are there days in your life when there seems no way? Are there nights when life seems a cross? On these lines, I'm going to invite you now into a meditative musical experience. While I sing this, you are free to close your eyes and just listen. Maybe keep the problem that you're facing at the back of your mind. Allow whatever message you get to emerge.

Figure 2
Scan the QR code to listen to "Hope, Faith, and Love."

Brain and Behavior Change

HOPE, FAITH, AND LOVE[19]

Is there something in your life that's not going right?
Is there something that you'd like to change?
Is there something in your life that makes no sense?
Do you feel like just giving up?
Are there times in your life when you had enough?
Are there times the clouds seem all black?
Are there days in your life when there seems no way?
Are there nights when life seems a cross?

Chorus:

>Hope, faith, and love's what keeps life moving on
>Hope, faith, and love, that's what life's all about
>Hope, faith, and love, my friend
>Will see us through

Yes, there were times in my life too
Days when I had enough
But hope just kept me going on
Hope in a God who loves

Chorus:

>Hope, faith, and love's what keeps life moving on
>Hope, faith, and love, that's what life's all about
>Hope, faith, and love, my friend
>Will see us through

PATHWAYS TO FREEDOM

We have discussed how chemical drugs affect the brain. We have moved on to behavioral addictions, which could be with devices, gambling, or the way one uses food. All behaviors use the same reward centers of the brain, as explained earlier. The question is now, what are the pathways to freedom? The way out of the addiction? I am going to offer some suggestions. Please note that the list is not exhaustive. Furthermore, from the vast array of mechanisms available, one has to choose a method that sits well within oneself. This will ensure the sustainability of this project of weaning ourselves away from our addiction.

1. Willpower. Primary in initiating a program of sobriety or abstinence is willpower. Sobriety is the complete giving up of that to which we are addicted, for example, alcohol or drugs. However, in the case of food and internet use, one cannot give it up completely. Hence, in such cases we speak of abstinence wherein we may choose how often and at what times we use the internet/check our phones/play video games. For initiating the pathway back to sobriety or abstinence, willpower is needed, but willpower soon reaches a plateau. All of us are aware of the phenomenon of "new year's resolutions." Most people begin with a lot of willpower and energy. But after a couple of weeks, the enthusiasm diminishes. Therefore, willpower is helpful as a runner's starting block, but it cannot be used for the long haul. Other strategies are necessary. Most of us would identify with the cravings of being on social media. "Check me! Check me!" calls out Facebook or WhatsApp. The craving to stop the work we are doing and get into these apps is real and intense. It is not just a psychological feeling that can be easily dismissed. The brain is actually asking for the next rush of dopamine and serotonin. So, the craving we have for food or drink, or for gambling, is very real. We need to recognize this because recognition or awareness is the first step toward healing. If we are able to override the serotonin and dopamine mediated midbrain commands, then we could be on the path to wholeness. The neuroscience of addiction helps us to trace our mechanisms, to transform the reinforcing pathways into long-term, adaptive changes.

2. Mind map your vision. A mind map is similar to a geographical map. It gives us a bird's-eye view of the area or the place where we want to visit. So, when talking about behavior change, we may want to make small improvements or sometimes large changes in many areas of our lives. All of these need to be put down on a piece of paper. It sometimes helps to write each point within a bubble or a conversation cloud. The circumference of this cloud will be bigger for big changes. Once we have mapped these clouds of differing sizes, we then choose one or two areas, at the most, which we can begin tackling in the coming weeks or months. It is not advisable to try and change everything about yourself all at once. Taking on too many goals at one time is also setting oneself up for failure. How do we discern which goal to choose from among the many goals that we have? The answer lies in listening to your body. In other words, you need to sense how much energy arising from your body is available to tackle a particular goal. The goal that excites you, or the one for which the body produces a lot of energy, is the one you should choose to tackle at this moment in time. It may not be the most important goal among the many that you have before you, but it is wise to wait for a later time until the energy arises to tackle that important goal.

3. Repeatedly place the thought in your mind. By repeatedly thinking of the new behavior that you are seeking to establish in your life, you enable more ideas to help that behavior get rooted. At the least, you should bring it to mind just before going to sleep and as soon as you get up in the morning. Other ways of bringing it to mind are by writing it down on paper, on sticky notes, on your cellphone screen, on flash cards, and on calendars. Make use of mnemonic devices. The mind tends to forget, therefore, the more you see your goal in front of you, the more likely your body and mind will start gravitating toward that behavior change. Very soon, it will become a natural extension of you.

4. Talk about it. One needs to talk about or express vocally the behavior one seeks to change. We are hesitant about sharing a goal that we have not yet achieved in our lives. What if we fail? Will our friends and family then make fun of us? These are natural negative thoughts that come to mind. But if we have the courage to have conversations about our goals, this is one more method of seeing them come to fruition. We can also speak about the difficulties we are facing and share our struggles with a close friend. If, for example, one of our goals is to be more sustainable and consume less, having conversations with those around us, as well as sharing our challenges, could motivate others to join in the task of slowing down climate change. Talking about it can even be on X (Twitter), Facebook, WhatsApp, or any other social media.

5. Be positive. Besides some of the physical steps outlined above, our mindset is key to attaining success. Psychologically, we need to be people of hope and faith. Our outlook should be positive despite the hiccups that may come our way. We have to remove the "im" from the impossible; we have to remove the "un" from the unable. A positive attitude in a person appears to attract positive results and brings greater chances of success. Positive language leads to positive thoughts and attitudes. This leads us to look for and appreciate the sometimes tiny positive influences in our lives. Furthermore, this gives us the enthusiasm to use those positive thoughts as launching pads to new ideas and experiences. Having a positive attitude is not just wishful thinking or being blind to the facts. It is a deliberate reframing of the perspective, which then creates a new enthusiasm for the task ahead.

6. Appeal to a higher power. We may be people of different religions or of no religion at all. Appealing to a higher power is one further step that helps us achieve our goals. In step 3, I spoke about repeatedly placing the thought in your mind. One can combine it with this step as a form of prayer, asking God to be with us in this venture when we say our prayers before going to bed and on waking up. There are some people who have had no experience of religion or spirituality growing up. There are others who have grown up within a religious denomination but have later made a 180-degree turn away from religion. Both these groups of people may find it difficult to appeal to a higher power. It is important that this appeal is not construed as having a whole new deity in front of us or a whole new set of rules and regulations. The operative word here is *belief*, not necessarily a fully laid out theology of that belief. Should I have an experience in order to believe? Or is it important to have belief as the first step after which an experience is bound to follow? The evidence arising from the success of a 12-step program and my own personal experience in working with people who have not had a faith background convinces me that appealing to a higher power contributes a significant amount to the process of behavior change. Even if I am a professed atheist, all that I need to do is choose to believe in something. I may not understand all of the contours of that belief, and yet it could be something that I choose to believe because belief works. For example, I may not understand how electricity works or all that goes into making electricity, but I know it works for me. Of course, those who are in an established belief system or religion have a greater support system that makes it easier to believe.

We began with painting a picture of different types of addiction. These could be broadly classified as substance and/or behavioral addictions. We have also looked at ways to bring about freedom from these addictions through behavior change. The steps outlined can be applied to achieving other goals of our life beyond just overcoming addictions. In addition to this methodology, the incorporation of Ignatian insights will aid the process of becoming a new person. Ignatian spirituality has been pursuing behavior change for five hundred years. The use of a combined neuro-psycho-Ignatian approach augurs well for sure success. Mindfulness, as explained in the next chapter, is a further tool to bring about behavior change.

5
JOURNEY TOWARD MINDFULNESS

MY FASCINATION WITH mindfulness began early in my teaching career. I was teaching a first-year chemistry class at St. Xavier's College in Mumbai, where the number of students in the class could be anywhere from 120 to 150. With such a large number it was difficult to get a silent atmosphere. Initially, I would get irritated at the constant murmur and lack of attention of the students. On further reflection, I realized that the chemistry class took place later in the day in their schedule. It was also quite likely that they would have attended three or four other science classes before showing up for my class, which would explain their distractedness. One day I suddenly stopped in between teaching the periodic table and invited them to experience a little mindfulness. I walked them through a brief mindfulness exercise for less than three minutes. After that, the whole class seemed much quieter and calmer. A few days later, I was surprised to receive the request for a mindfulness exercise from the students themselves. They had been hooked, realizing for themselves the benefits of mindfulness.

Journey toward Mindfulness

MEDITATION AS AWARENESS

In chapter 2, I mentioned that meditation can be divided into two types: concentrative and awareness. There I had also listed steps to meditate using the concentrative technique, focusing on the breath. While in many instances the words *meditation* and *mindfulness* are used interchangeably, I would like to use the term *mindfulness* for the awareness aspect of meditation. Mindfulness is the practice of being aware of your mind, body, and feelings in the present moment, which is thought to create a feeling of calm (see dictionary.cambridge.org). My journey with mindfulness began with a ten-day retreat called Vipassana that focuses on the breath for the first three days ("anapana") and then doing body awareness exercises with very little consumption of food. I witnessed firsthand the power of the mind over the body. It was only natural, then, that when it was time to begin my doctoral studies, I wanted to do it in neuroscience, which studies the brain and its chemistry, creating a smooth transition from chemistry to neuroscience. During my doctoral studies, I had the good fortune to do a one-semester course in mind-body medicine at Harvard University. My area of research was meditation. But for me, all my studies were indirectly aimed at how to move the human person toward higher levels of human flourishing. The verse from John 10:10 is my personal mantra: "I have come that you may have life and life in abundance." And so, all my studies, whether in chemistry, neuroscience, or consciousness, were toward that goal.

While I was doing my doctoral studies in Boston, I had the opportunity to attend the Society of Neuroscience Annual Conference in Washington, D.C., which had in attendance the Dalai Lama. He was invited there by neuroscientist Dr. Richard Davidson. Through that conference, I saw firsthand how the

UNITING MIND, BODY, SPIRIT

Dalai Lama is constantly working to build a happy, peaceful world through mindfulness. He strongly encourages the use of science and research on mindfulness to meet this end. I later attended a summer program on mindfulness conducted by Dr. Davidson at a beautiful retreat house in Garrison, New York. Dr. Davidson was a big influence on me during the early days of my doctoral studies.

Mindfulness is nothing but paying attention to the matter at hand, being aware, and living in the present moment. (It will come as no surprise that the beginning of my thesis is titled "The Chemistry of Attention.") But most of us are aware that this is easier said than done. It is the nature of the mind to either remain in the past having regrets or guilt, or else jump to the future, worried and anxious. To remain in the present moment, it is important to strain out all that is irrelevant and to prepare us for what we need to do next. This job is done by the brain stem and the subcortical regions. Data coming in from our perception/awareness is integrated by the primary sensory cortices at the surface of the brain. Later, assessment is done in the prefrontal cortex. Besides individual episodes of awareness, from time to time we need to do a meta-awareness, which is evaluating where our attention is at any given moment and where it is going to be. In simple words, it is thinking about thinking. This meta-awareness provides us with an insight into any habit that we form in life that results in our overall behavior. The Dhammapada, one of the sacred texts of Buddhism, contains the following line: "Our life is shaped by our mind for we become what we think."[1]

Therefore, it is important to be in touch with what is going on in our minds as well as in our bodies and our spirits, too. For good health, as discussed in chapter 2, we need to consider mind, body, and the spirit as one complete entity. A few points bear repetition. St. Ignatius of Loyola strongly emphasized repetition, and neuroscience demonstrates its usefulness. Thanks to medical sciences and bioengineering we have made quantum leaps in treating disease and physical accidents. We can now put in a titanium plate for a fracture. We can do a joint organ transfer, transplanting the heart and the lung from one donor to a recipient. We can do almost anything now with stem cell research and genome mapping. We have made enormous leaps with repairing the body. When it comes to the mind, we have made progress, but we still have a long way to go in establishing scientifically verifiable protocols for treatments and cures. Psychiatry today relies very much on chemical drugs. As a chemist myself, I don't want to sound as if I am downplaying the work of chemistry in bringing relief to patients with mental health problems. Drugs offer an immediate solution to a hyperactive child, who may be causing a disturbance in a classroom. But have we studied the long-term effects of pumping Ritalin continuously into a child who has ADHD? Would there be long-term personality changes brought about due to this continuous infusion of chemicals into the young body? Drugs for depression and mood elevation may help in the short term. However, one fears we are treating the symptoms rather than the problem. While there have been benefits, there are a lot of ethical issues when dealing with the mind and how we treat the problems of the mind.

Let us move onto the realm of the spirit. With wars fought over religion and the use of religious texts to justify racism, discrimination and exclusivity, and other such aberrations, the world of the spirit has been neglected. This is a clear case of throwing out the baby with the bathwater. Another reason for ignoring the spirit has been the overreliance on the whole scientific method where we look for proofs, double-blind trials, and replicability. We believe that science can explain everything about human experience. We forget that science works on boundary conditions, and once we establish those boundaries, all our answers will be found within those boundaries. Science understands this very acutely. Thus, science is very careful about not making statements or predictions about that which is outside the boundary conditions. The triumphalist position of science as king of knowledge comes more from the media and the general public. A true scientist who delves deeper and deeper into the subject awakens each morning with the humbling realization of, in fact, how scanty one's knowledge is and how much more one needs to know.

THE BODY-MIND CONNECTION

So, we once again reiterate the importance of the mind, body, and spirit when we are looking at the well-being of the whole person. Ignatian spirituality looks at these three elements together. In an earlier chapter, we established the three nervous systems, how the body affects the mind, and how the mind affects the body. It is as simple as when I'm nervous, I get butterflies in my stomach. Or for young kids, they feel the urge to use the restroom often. The mind affects the body in so many ways. For years it was thought that the immune system was protected. Nothing could affect it from the outside. Today, we know that that is not true. What happens in the mind also affects the body/immune system. But when we go to an alternate question, "Does the body affect the mind?" the seminal study on the brains of taxi drivers in London that we discussed in the earlier chapters gives us an affirmative answer to that.

The body can affect the mind, as we say, psychologically, but new research demonstrates an actual physiological change in the brain. We are now also aware of the concept of adult neurogenesis, the formation of new neuronal connections and pathways even in the adult brain. For centuries, it was believed that our brains are fixed from early childhood, but today we know that we can have new neural connections growing at least in some parts of the brain.[2] Therefore, if you want to stave off Alzheimer's or dementia, you need to keep the brain active by keeping it engaged. My favorite line is, "It is possible to learn to play the piano even at the age of sixty!" We in academia think we are using our minds constantly because we are teaching and researching every second day, but most of us teach what we learned during our master's and doctoral programs, and then add a little more along the way. So, we are not forming new neuronal connections; we are just using the old ones. Therefore, to keep the mind activated one must do brain exercises like Sudoku or crosswords, learn a new language, or learn a new skill. One could also dust off that old guitar from twenty years back and learn to play it again. Allowing the brain to create new cells keeps us active and alive. In summary, the mind affects the body, and the body affects the brain. The question of distinction between mind and brain is a huge field in philosophy.

One potent tool to help build new patterns in the brain or rearrange the old ones is mindfulness, as I have mentioned earlier. I reiterate the importance of mindfulness as being aware and living in the present moment. However, the mind either sits in the past or loves to jump into the future. If it is in the past, the emotions accompanying it can be guilt, regret, or sadness. "I could have done this differently," and "I should have taken the other path." Then the mind jumps into the future. "I am worried, I am fearful, and I am anxious about what is to come." The nature of the mind is to resist being rooted in the present. Through mindfulness, we are trying to keep the mind in the present. When we are in the now, our actions, our alertness, and our awareness get sharper. Mindfulness goes hand in hand with thinking about thinking or meta-awareness.[3]

It is important to be in touch with what is going on in our bodies and our minds. When we face a negative emotion, we need to first become aware of it, pay attention to it, allow it to rise to the surface, and then let it dissipate. We would need to do this several times before we can hopefully get rid of those strong negative emotions or at least lessen their hold over us. Our negative emotions could be, as mentioned earlier, regret, guilt, anger, fear, anxiety, and so forth. Plenty of research shows that these could be high-risk factors for a heart attack, depression, and aging. Research also shows that anger, fear, anxiety, and sadness weaken our immune system as well as cause atrophy of certain areas of the brain responsible for regulating such emotions. Thus, we end up in a spiral of increasing negative emotions. Dr. David Vago has researched female patients suffering from fibromyalgia,[4] which is associated with widespread muscular tenderness, chronic pain, and a host of other symptoms. These patients had a high level of anxiety and fear associated with their pain. Mindfulness training was offered to them. The outcome was a remarkable reduction in their clinical symptoms. The patients were given a behavioral task that assessed how they paid attention to pain-related words (*devastating, distressing, aching, tender, pulsating, sore, pounding*) at their nonconscious perceptual level and the more conscious evaluative level.

The untrained patients avoided those words at the nonconscious perceptual level, whereas the ones trained in mindfulness focused on the words. This suggested that the trained patients had less fear and avoidance and more approach-related behavior toward their pain. This is a stage of processing wherein they didn't have any awareness of what they were doing. The untrained group also had the tendency to ruminate, whereas their counterparts had the capacity to let pain go easily. This shows us that mindfulness training can improve our mental habits of attention at both the conscious and nonconscious levels.

TO EXTRACT, TO IMPLANT, AND TO BOND

We have explored the concept of mindfulness and pointed out some evidence of the mechanism behind it. Putting it into actual practice is best done by using a saying from dentistry: to extract, to implant, and to bond.

To extract is to remove the baggage that each one of us carries in our interactions with one another as well as baggage or biases or stereotypes that exist between communities. We need to extract painful memories, hurt feelings, perceived insults, and other negativities that live in our consciousness. We cannot do this with just willpower or strong determination. We need a systematic method. Second, we need to implant the advantages of letting go of our baggage. One important tool is to implant a different perspective into our thinking. Third, we must experience in our imagination the freedom and joy that comes from being unencumbered by baggage. The light feeling and the relief that comes about is like no other. The imagery that would help is that of a schoolboy who as soon as he reaches home throws the backpack from his shoulder. Relief! We should allow the new way of thinking to cement itself onto our brain so that the bond may become a permanent one and we can be free of our baggage.

The above is applicable to personal relationships, doctor-patient relationships, as well as relationships between a racial group and the health-care system. We can use this three-step process in our endeavor to be antiracist, let's say, and factor the social determinants of health into the health-care system. This is necessary to extract the evil of racism from systems where it is embedded, hidden from view, in order to implant an equitable system that allows for people from disadvantaged backgrounds to get a leg up. When groups have opportunities to know one another, to allow dialogue to take place, and to attempt to heal past wounds, this will ensure that bonding takes place.

Mindfulness as a practical tool is helpful to be serene and calm in approaching the ups and downs of everyday living. When this is combined with aspects of Ignatian spirituality, it helps to bring us closer to human flourishing in a shorter period. The technique of Discernment of Spirits can begin with a quieting of the mind through the practice of mindfulness. We can then place before ourselves that which is to be discerned. I have covered in detail Discernment of Spirits in chapter 3.

Mindfulness is not just about solving our personal issues or "navel gazing." It is also helpful in becoming aware of broader societal issues. Currently, we have been made aware of how discrimination based on race, gender, religion, and so forth, is not just an individual issue but is embedded in systems of governance, the judiciary, and in the workplace. Oftentimes, we are not aware of our own biases until someone points them out to us and we think about them. That is also a part of meditation and being mindful: looking at yourself from the outside. Attempts to reduce the glaring inequalities have been made by the realization that to be truly fair to all we have to begin by leveling the playing field. The concept of equity allows us to ensure that a deserving person is given an extra step to stand on so that they can also enjoy the view. Thus, the concept of equity makes more sense than just talking about equality or merit.

AN EXERCISE IN MINDFULNESS

I would like to end this chapter by offering you an exercise in mindfulness. The steps are below.

Figure 3
Scan the QR code to hear the Guided Mindfulness Meditation.

Journey toward Mindfulness

I invite you to join me in a mindfulness meditation.

1. Sit in a comfortable posture, either on a chair or cross-legged on the floor. The main goal is to keep the spine erect, but don't tense yourself up in trying to do so. The whole body needs to be relaxed yet alert.
2. Keep your hands open in front of you with both palms facing upward, or you may want to join your hands at the fingertips in the shape of a heart, like a semi-praying position.
3. Now that the body is ready, let us take a few deep breaths. As you breathe out, breathe out as if you are sighing. Allow yourself to let go of the stresses and tensions of the day. Breath out a couple of times, and each time as you breathe out, feel the body relax. With the body now relaxed, return to your normal breathing.
4. This mindfulness-awareness exercise is going to use the scanning technique, just as if we were in a CT scan, which scans horizontal slices of the body from head to toe. In the same way, we are going to use our mind to scan the body from head to toe.
5. Become aware of the top of your head, then slowly move your awareness to your forehead. Expand the skin on your forehead and face by keeping the face in a gentle smile.
6. Become aware of your eyes. Allow the eyeballs to recede deep into the eye sockets as if falling asleep.
7. Become aware of your nose...your lips...your chin...and your neck. If you notice a sensation, stay with it for a second and then move on to the next area. Do not attempt to identify the sensation or give it a name. Just be aware of it and move on.

UNITING MIND, BODY, SPIRIT

Know that you are totally relaxed, totally calm as you scan the body.
8. Next we will move slowly to our shoulders…arms…forearms…wrists, and fingers. Feel the whole hands relaxing and aware.
9. Then bring your awareness to your chest…your stomach…your upper back, including the area just below your shoulders…your lower back.
10. Then lower your awareness to your hips…your thighs.…If you notice any sensation, just become aware of it, and let it go. Return to focusing your awareness on your body as you scan it layer by layer. We now move to our knees…and then the calves…and then the ankles…and finally our feet.
11. Stay a moment with this awareness of the lower part of the body. Now stay a moment with an awareness of the whole body as one united whole.
12. Then begin again with the top of the head and follow the same pattern of scanning every section of the body. If you note a sensation, acknowledge it, and then move on.
13. I will be in silence as I give you the time to scan your body once again.
14. Remember if a distracting thought comes, acknowledge it, tell it that you will attend to it later. Then return to your awareness exercise.
15. It does not matter how often you get distracting thoughts; the aim is to catch them sooner than later and return to your mindfulness.
16. This process can be repeated many times. Always perform it with ease and feel the relaxation it brings. As you get more comfortable with it, you can increase the length of time that you spend in mindfulness. It is never a waste. It charges you for

the remaining part of the day, and improves your concentration, so that which needed one hour can be done in half the time.
17. At the end of the mindfulness meditation, wait for a few minutes before standing up. Also, don't get up abruptly for a phone call or a knock. The body is very relaxed and needs time to come into active mode.

　　Treat yourself to mindfulness every day, even if for a brief while. The body thanks you.

6

LET'S GROW TOGETHER
Further Ignatian Insights

IN THIS FINAL chapter, we lay out important aspects of Ignatian spirituality necessary for everyday living. These can be applied in multiple contexts whether it be sitting in the classroom, writing a play or poem, or planning an event.

THE IMPORTANCE OF CONTEXT

One aspect of Ignatian spirituality that is very much emphasized is "context." Context has to be considered in every situation that we are in whether it be in education or more broadly in life in general. I will take education as an example to work with as most people are familiar with that environment. Feel free to adapt to your work or community situation if it applies. In a school setup, within each discipline, context is important if we are going to make an impact. An average teacher dictates good notes, which help the students in their exams. A good teacher challenges the students to think and encourages different points of view, both assent and dissent. An excellent teacher inspires students and, like the mother eagle, incites them to fly out of the comfort of the nest when she considers them ready. Thus, the motto for many Jesuit institutions is *Provocans ad Volandum*—"provoking to fly."

If education is to be relevant and useful, no longer confined to an ivory tower, it has to descend into the lives of ordinary people. The question that we must constantly ask ourselves is, "Am I MAD?" This means, "Am I Making A Difference?" No matter what subject we teach, whether it is humanities, social sciences, or pure sciences, we have to situate it in a context. So, even if I am in the field of entomology (insects), and I am studying not all but just one group of insects called Coleoptera (beetles), I, as a coleopterist, must be concerned about ecology and the safeguarding of the environment. I am aware that every creature has a role to play, a niche to fill in the cycle of life (let's forget mosquitoes for the time being!). It is indeed easier to bring in the context for the humanities and social sciences, but that does not absolve those of us in the sciences from doing the same. If you are an educator, in whichever field, to bring in the context of the students whom we serve is even more imperative. This contextual relevance will inspire us and motivate us to be selfless human beings.

To better use this concept of context, one must answer three questions:

- Who is the audience?
- Who am I as the speaker?
- What is the medium for communication?

The first question regarding context is: Who is the audience? Who are my students? Am I aware of their backgrounds and the fact that I may be teaching a very heterogeneous class? The students may come into the program with different levels of science background. Furthermore, their living situations will be varied. Some may have to manage a home and children, and some may have to take care of aged parents. Either of these scenarios will affect the time available for their academic work.

The second question regarding context is: Who am I? What is my current environment, whether at home or in the department where I teach? Am I a new teacher or have I been doing this for years? What is the level of enthusiasm that I bring to the class? Do I have the time to incorporate the latest research into my teaching?

The third question: What is the medium that I am going to use to convey my knowledge as well as my experience in health care to my students? In an age of attention deficit, minimum concentrative ability, and the need for different techniques to keep the young mind engaged, what are the tools that I have in my chalk box/Zoom box as an educator?

Using these steps will ensure that we are trying to be relevant to our audience. The process has integrity because we are speaking from our genuine selves, and we have determined the appropriate medium of communication.

FREEDOM IS OUR GOAL

The goal of Ignatian spirituality is to make oneself increasingly free through union and communion with the divine. We all need liberation; we all need to be free. We need freedom from enslavement to gadgets, to name, fame, and wealth. Freedom from systems and practices that have passed their expiration date. St. Ignatius of Loyola was revolutionary in his thinking. While most religious organizations at that time placed their emphasis on praying many times during the day in choir, he abolished this rule because he wanted his men to be out in the field laboring with the masses. We need freedom from dealing with unimaginable illnesses that lead to broken bodies and destroyed lives, freedom from assaults, attacks that result in "humanity gone, justice crushed."[1] In most cases, it is the poor who bear the brunt of it. Our earth longs for healing, our world needs love. Freedom "from" is not enough because a person may get free from all baggage and be in a balanced state of mind yet not have an enthusiasm for a life lived fully. Thus, freedom "for" is important. Freedom for making this world a better place, a heaven on earth, and for bringing about the kingdom of God or a *Ram Rajya* here on earth itself. In many different religious scriptures, God says, "I want justice not sacrifice, not burnt offerings nor gifts but repentant hearts ready for reconciliation" (see Hos 6:6). Thus, both freedom "from" and freedom "for" allow us to be healed. We as parents, educators, and global citizens are in a privileged place to provide that healing and love not only to our children and our students but to all those in need. As people who are healed, we are called to face the challenge of our times and disturb the inequalities in our systems. Doing this will ensure a more equitable society in which the fruits of progress are made available to all. I invite you to immerse yourself in this composition of mine, "The Challenge."

Figure 4
Scan the QR code to listen to "The Challenge."

THE CHALLENGE[2]

Broken bodies, lives destroyed
But unbroken in spirit
Humanity gone, justice crushed
The poor bear the brunt of it all

UNITING MIND, BODY, SPIRIT

Chorus:
>Lord, our earth longs for healing
>Lord, the world needs your love
>To face the challenge, disturb the rich
>And comfort all the poor

Broken bodies, lives destroyed
But unbroken in spirit
Humanity gone, justice crushed
The poor bear the brunt of it all

Chorus:
>Lord, our earth longs for healing
>Lord, the world needs your love
>To face the challenge, disturb the rich
>And comfort all the poor

Liberation, the world needs it
We all need to be free
Freedom from enslavement,
Freedom for the Kingdom of God

Chorus:
>Lord, our earth longs for healing
>Lord, the world needs your love
>To face the challenge, disturb the rich
>And comfort all the poor

I want justice, not sacrifice
Not burnt offerings nor gifts
Repentant hearts, contrite souls
A spirit that is free

Let's Grow Together

Chorus:

>Lord, our earth longs for healing
>Lord, the world needs your love
>To face the challenge, disturb the rich
>And comfort all the poor

Sometimes looking at the context, it is only natural to feel dejected, downcast, or even cynical. Why should I bother to change the world? Can one person make a difference? And so, it is necessary to have the right attitude. We have heard so much about positive thinking and the need to look at the brighter side of life. It is not just a cliché but involves making repeated choices to remove the negative thinking that keeps popping up in our minds and replace it with positive affirmations that this can be done, this situation can be overcome, and I can do it! Remember, the mind abhors a vacuum. Thus, just trying to push away negative thinking will not help. We have to replace the negative thoughts with a positive statement. Our belief has to be that the outcome we are hoping for in our situation is going to take place. The phrase "Believe it till you achieve it" is powerful. The brain, at some level, cannot distinguish between "doing" an action and "imagining" that we are doing that action. There is research to prove this, but before reading about this research I experienced this in my own life intuitively. When I entered in college, I participated in piano auditions to be the one performer who would represent St. Xavier's College at the annual intercollegiate Malhar festival. Someone else was chosen, but two weeks before the competition I was informed that the person chosen had stepped down and that I, as the runner-up, would represent the college. I had just two weeks to prepare a complicated piano piece alongside my daily classes and the two-hour commute between home and college. I used most of the commute time on the bus to study this score of music while playing on an imaginary piano placed on my lap. The only real practice I got on the piano was a little time at night. At the end of it all, I did very well at the competition.

Much later, while doing my neuroscience studies, I came upon some research that had two groups of students who were given a score of music and told to come prepared to play it in about two weeks.[3] However, one group had no access to a piano during that time. It was found that the performance of the ones who did not have access to the piano earlier was only slightly below that of the other group who had access to the piano. The experiment was repeated, and the second time around the students who did not have piano access during the two weeks were allowed one hour of practice time before the competition. This time the performance of both the groups was on par. This demonstrated that going through the score in one's mind and playing it on an imaginary piano, as I did many years earlier, is almost as good as practicing on an actual piano. Doing is important but imagining doing is a big help as well. You have to "believe it till you achieve it." The best antidote to giving into cynicism and depression, throwing up one's hands in despair is the firm belief that no matter how dark a circumstance is or how long the night is, the sun will come out tomorrow. There will be light.

AN EXAMINATION OF CONSCIOUSNESS

Another important tool for mindfulness is the attitude of gratitude. We can look back at the years that have gone by in our own lives and know that our higher power has somehow seen us through many difficult situations. We have gone through valleys and mountains. To reach the next mountain peak, it is sometimes necessary to traverse a valley. We have much to be grateful for in our everyday lives, if only we look around and become aware of it. Once aware, we can give thanks and move through the day with a grateful heart.

Awareness of the past and our accomplishments elicits an attitude of gratitude. But to be mindful involves a constant awareness of our present. We are invited to constantly check in on ourselves to see how our day is going and how we are feeling. The examination of consciousness, or the examen, in short, is help offered by St. Ignatius, not so much to discover times we were able to seek God but to recall where God has encountered us. It includes spending about ten to fifteen minutes before lunch and at night before going to bed scanning through the events of the day and becoming aware of our ups and downs, or as St. Ignatius puts it, our consolations and desolations. We do not make a judgment on them but just observe. Most importantly, we try to detect God's presence in our lives through all the events. The following steps may be helpful.

1. Begin with an act of surrender, a prayer, or some quiet time. This could be in the form of a brief meditation for two minutes.
2. Give thanks to God for the gift of being alive and for all that has happened to you during the day.
3. Begin scanning through the day from the time you got up till the present moment. It is as if you are seeing your day go by on a television screen. Don't judge, just observe. Be aware of any feelings arising.
4. Listen to what your inner voice is trying to tell you as you scan through the day. Where is God in all this?
5. End with a prayer of gratitude.

The intent of this prayer is not to be an exercise in beating ourselves up for the times we failed. Thus, the examination of conscience is now more commonly referred to as the examination of consciousness because the focus is encountering God in all things.

MINDFULNESS AND THE *MAGIS*

Mindfulness calls for being sensitive to the situation we are in. What is the mood of the person I am dealing with at the present moment, be it a student, colleague, patient, or client? What is the energy level of those with whom I am working? It also calls for us to be sensitive to our own disposition. While mindfulness does call for sensitivity to the situation, the practice of mindfulness itself sharpens our sensitivity in general. You can detect feelings and emotions in the room. You are also able to pick up clues that you would have missed prior to mindfulness practice. You are able to sense when something is beginning to unravel and can take quick steps to remedy the situation.

In Ignatian spirituality, the word *Magis* is an important concept that translates as "the better" or "the more." St. Ignatius does not speak of "the best" or "the most" but in all that we do, he invites us to seek out the more. The "more" of St. Ignatius does not have the same meaning as "more" in our consumeristic society. Once we get an idea of what our particular mission in this world is, we need to give it our full effort. It is very easy today either at the workplace or at home, to have a sort of laissez-faire attitude or a *chalta hai* mentality. But mediocrity does not get us far. The *Magis* does not mean that we are constantly comparing ourselves to others. It is more of comparing yourself with yourself and each time trying to push the limits of your talents, skills, and competencies. I would like to offer you this song for meditation that I composed based on the theme of the *Magis*. Read the lyrics first, and become aware of the thoughts and feelings evoked within you.

Let's Grow Together

Figure 5
Scan the QR code to listen to "Going beyond the Stars."

GOING BEYOND THE STARS[4]

I feel it deep within me
But I can't put it in words
An urging draws me near
And yet it's not so clear
To go beyond the furthest shore
And climb the tallest peak
But the path's not there at all
So, what if I should fall

Chorus:

> Going beyond the stars above
> Crossing mighty seas
> Dreaming the impossible dream
> And seeing it through till the end

To do something meaningful
With this life, I've been called
But which for me is the way
Know, not I, to this day

Chorus:

> Going beyond the stars above
> Changing wrong to right

UNITING MIND, BODY, SPIRIT

Fighting for a worthy cause
And seeing it through till the end

Going beyond the stars above
Crossing mighty seas
Dreaming the impossible dream
And seeing it through till the end

CONCLUSION

Health is one of the most important elements in our lives. Wealth, fame, and name cannot be pursued at the expense of health. Health is the tripartite combination of body, mind, and spirit. It is only when all these three are addressed together can one achieve flourishing. Being in good health helps us tackle times of uncertainty, rapid change, and crisis from a much better vantage point. Good health helps a person be more resilient to face the knocks that life hits us with. The spirituality of St. Ignatius is a handy guidebook during difficult times. In particular, his "Discernment of Spirits" has been a method that has stood the test of time. Combining the insights of St. Ignatius with the findings of recent neuroscience research helps us to bring about the behavior change we desire in our lives, but we need to remember that this is a slow process, and we need to be patient. The change will come but maybe not as fast as we would want it to. At all times, we must keep in mind the aim of behavior change is ultimately to make a difference in the world. The outcome is true happiness—for ourselves and everyone around us.

NOTES

CHAPTER 1

1. CDC, "1918 Pandemic Influenza Historic Timeline," Center for Disease Control and Prevention, March 20, 2018, accessed January 14, 2022, https://www.cdc.gov/flu/pandemic-resources/1918-commemoration/pandemic-timeline-1918.htm.

2. P. Spreeuwenberg, M. Kroneman, and J. Paget, "Reassessing the Global Mortality Burden of the 1918 Influenza Pandemic," *American Journal of Epidemiology* 187, no. 12 (2018): 2561–67, https://doi.org/10.1093/aje/kwy191.

3. D. He, S. Zhao, Y. Li, P. Cao, D. Gao, Y. Lou, and L. Yang, "Comparing COVID-19 and the 1918–19 Influenza Pandemics in the United Kingdom," *International Journal of Infectious Diseases* 98 (2020): 67–70, https://doi.org/10.1016/j.ijid.2020.06.075.

4. I. C. Campbell, "Zoom Events Will Try to Re-Create the In-Person Conference Experience," The Verge, May 19, 2021, accessed January 17, 2022, https://www.theverge.com/2021/5/19/22442919/zoom-live-events-paid-tickets-conferences-chat.

5. G. Pietrabissa and S. G. Simpson, "Psychological Consequences of Social Isolation during COVID-19 Outbreak," *Frontiers in Psychology* 11 (2020), https://doi.org/10.3389/fpsyg.2020.02201.

6. C. del Rio and P. Malani, "COVID-19 in 2021—Continuing Uncertainty," *JAMA* 325, no. 14 (2021): 1389–90, https://doi.org/10.1001/jama.2021.3760.

7. M. J. Laskey, "A Cannonball Strike Kept Saint Ignatius Stuck in Bed. Thank God for That," Jesuits.Org., May 21, 2020, accessed January 18, 2022, https://www.jesuits.org/stories/a-cannonball-strike-kept-saint-ignatius-stuck-in-bed-thank-god-for-that/.

8. Ignatius (Vita 1) as quoted in W. W. Meissner, *Ignatius of Loyola: The Psychology of a Saint* (New Haven, CT: Yale University Press, 1992), 35.

9. Meissner, *Ignatius of Loyola*, 35.

10. Meissner, *Ignatius of Loyola*, 45.

11. I. O. Loyola and L. J. Puhl, *The Spiritual Exercises of St. Ignatius: Based on Studies in the Language of the Autograph*, 1st ed. (Chicago: Loyola Press, 1968).

12. Meissner, *Ignatius of Loyola*, 177.

13. C. G. Nauert, "The Clash of Humanists and Scholastics: An Approach to Pre-Reformation Controversies," *Sixteenth Century Journal* 4, no. 1 (1973): 1–18, https://doi.org/10.2307/2539764.

14. Ignatius (Vita 8) as quoted in W. W. Meissner, *Ignatius of Loyola: The Psychology of a Saint* (New Haven, CT: Yale University Press, 1992), 47.

15. E. Khantzian and J. E. Mack, "Self-Preservation and the Care of the Self," *The Psychoanalytic Study of the Child* 38, no. 1 (1983): 209–32, https://doi.org/10.1080/00797308.1983.11823390.

CHAPTER 2

1. J. M. Grinyo, "Why Is Organ Transplantation Clinically Important?" *Cold Spring Harbor Perspectives in Medicine* 3, no. 6 (2013): a014985, https://doi.org/10.1101/cshperspect.a014985.

Notes

2. C. Karch, C. Cruchaga, and A. Goate, "Alzheimer's Disease Genetics: From the Bench to the Clinic," *Neuron* 83, no. 1 (2014): 11–26, https://doi.org/10.1016/j.neuron.2014.05.041.

3. R. Harland, E. Antonova, G. S. Owen, M. Broome, S. Landau, Q. Deeley, and R. Murray, "A Study of Psychiatrists' Concepts of Mental Illness," *Psychological Medicine* 39, no. 6 (2008): 967–76, https://doi.org/10.1017/s0033291708004881; J. Moncrieff and D. Cohen, "How Do Psychiatric Drugs Work?" *BMJ* 338 (May 29, 2009): b1963, https://doi.org/10.1136/bmj.b1963.

4. R. Pereira and J. Kozhamthadam, *The Human Soul in a World of the Neurological Sciences* (New Delhi: Indian Society for Promoting Christian Knowledge, 2021), 66.

5. Y. B. Lee, J. Yu, H. H. Choi, B. S. Jeon, H. K. Kim, S. W. Kim, S. S. Kim, Y. G. Park, and H. S. Chae, "The Association between Peptic Ulcer Diseases and Mental Health Problems," *Medicine* 96, no. 34 (2017): e7828, https://doi.org/10.1097/md.0000000000007828.

6. E. A. Maguire, K. Woollett, and H. J. Spiers, "London Taxi Drivers and Bus Drivers: A Structural MRI and Neuropsychological Analysis," *Hippocampus* 16, no. 12 (2006): 1091–101, https://doi.org/10.1002/hipo.20233.

7. R. J. Davidson, J. Kabat-Zinn, J. Schumacher, M. Rosenkranz, D. Muller, S. F. Santorelli, F. Urbanowski, A. Harrington, K. Bonus, and J. F. Sheridan, "Alterations in Brain and Immune Function Produced by Mindfulness Meditation," *Psychosomatic Medicine* 65, no. 4 (2003): 564–70, https://doi.org/10.1097/01.psy.0000077505.67574.e3.

8. R. Pereira, "Meditation and Beyond: Phenomena Beyond Materialism," (lecture, Cosmos, Nature and Culture: A Transdisciplinary Conference, Phoenix, AZ, July 2010).

9. T. L. Goldsby, M. E. Goldsby, M. McWalters, and P. J. Mills, "Effects of Singing Bowl Sound Meditation on Mood, Tension, and Well-being: An Observational Study," *Journal of*

Evidence-Based Complementary and Alternative Medicine 22, no. 3 (2016): 401–6, https://doi.org/10.1177/2156587216668109.

10. D. Raab, "Calming the Monkey Mind: Do You Have an Inner Voice That Hinders Your Success?" *Psychology Today*, September 13, 2017, accessed January 22, 2022, https://www.psychologytoday.com/us/blog/the-empowerment-diary/201709/calming-the-monkey-mind.

11. R. E. Beaty, P. Seli, and D. L. Schacter, "Thinking about the Past and Future in Daily Life: An Experience Sampling Study of Individual Differences in Mental Time Travel," *Psychological Research* 83, no. 4 (2018): 805–16, https://doi.org/10.1007/s00426-018-1075-7.

CHAPTER 3

1. Personal correspondence, January 23, 2022. For further reference, see Paul Coutinho, SJ, *How Big Is Your God? The Freedom to Experience the Divine* (Chicago: Loyola Press, 2010).

2. W. W. Meissner, *Ignatius of Loyola: The Psychology of a Saint* (New Haven, CT: Yale University Press, 1992), 61–62.

CHAPTER 4

1. A. T. McLellan, "Substance Misuse and Substance Use Disorders: Why Do They Matter in Healthcare?" *Transactions of the American Clinical and Climatological Association* 128 (2017): 112–30.

2. U.S. Department of Health and Human Services (HHS), Office of the Surgeon General, "Facing Addiction in America: The Surgeon General's Report on Alcohol, Drugs, and Health" (Washington, DC: HHS, November 2016).

3. National Institute on Drug Abuse (NIDA), "Drugs and the Brain," July 27, 2021, accessed January 25, 2022, https://www

.drugabuse.gov/publications/drugs-brains-behavior-science-addiction/drugs-brain.

    4. A. L. Frederick and G. D. Stanwood, "Drugs, Biogenic Amine Targets and the Developing Brain," *Developmental Neuroscience* 31, no. 1–2 (2009): 7–22, https://doi.org/10.1159/000207490.

    5. N. D. Volkow, J. S. Fowler, G. J. Wang, and J. M. Swanson, "Dopamine in Drug Abuse and Addiction: Results from Imaging Studies and Treatment Implications," *Molecular Psychiatry* 9, no. 6 (2004): 557–69, https://doi.org/10.1038/sj.mp.4001507.

    6. V. Woollaston, "Generation Mobile Zombie: 1 in 10 Look at Their Phone As Soon As They Wake Up—And Almost 50% of People Check Their Mobile Phone at Least 50 Times a Day," Daily Mail.com, September 8, 2015b, accessed January 28, 2022, https://www.dailymail.co.uk/sciencetech/article-3226070/Generation-mobile-zombie-1-10-look-phone-soon-wake-50-check-50-times-day.html.

    7. L. E. Frank, A. R. Preston, and D. Zeithamova, "Functional Connectivity between Memory and Reward Centers across Task and Rest Track Memory Sensitivity to Reward," *Cognitive, Affective & Behavioral Neuroscience* 19, no. 3 (2019): 503–22, https://doi.org/10.3758/s13415-019-00700-8.

    8. S. Srinahyanti, Y. Wau, I. Manurung, and N. Arjani, "Influence of Gadget: A Positive and Negative Impact of Smartphone Usage for Early Child," *Proceedings of the 2nd Annual Conference of Engineering and Implementation on Vocational Education (ACEIVE 2018), 3rd November 2018, North Sumatra, Indonesia*, EAI (2019), https://doi.org/10.4108/eai.3-11-2018.2285692.

    9. K. Kumar and S. Allarakha, "What Is the Normal Range for IQ? Chart," MedicineNet, March 4, 2021b, accessed January 28, 2022, https://www.medicinenet.com/what_is_the_normal_range_for_iq/article.htm.

10. E. A. Maguire, K. Woollett, and H. J. Spiers, "London Taxi Drivers and Bus Drivers: A Structural MRI and Neuropsychological Analysis," *Hippocampus* 16, no. 12 (2006): 1091–101, https://doi.org/10.1002/hipo.20233.

11. D. Mosher, "High Wired: Does Addictive Internet Use Restructure the Brain?" *Scientific American*, June 17, 2011, accessed January 28, 2022, https://www.scientificamerican.com/article/does-addictive-internet-use-restructure-brain/.

12. A. Weinstein, L. Curtiss Feder, K. P. Rosenberg, and P. Dannon, "Internet Addiction Disorder," *Behavioral Addictions* (2014): 99–117, https://doi.org/10.1016/b978-0-12-407724-9.00005-7.

13. J. Harris, "How the Internet Is Altering Your Mind," *The Guardian*, November 25, 2017, accessed January 28, 2022, https://www.theguardian.com/technology/2010/aug/20/internet-altering-your-mind#:%7E:text=As%20Small%20put%20it%3A%20%22After,had%20already%20rewired%20their%20brains.%22.

14. C. T. S. U. S. McCarthy-Jones, "Are Social Networking Sites Controlling Your Mind?" *Scientific American*, December 8, 2017, accessed January 28, 2022, https://www.scientificamerican.com/article/are-social-networking-sites-controlling-your-mind/.

15. Wellcome Trust, "Number of Facebook Friends Linked to Size of Brain Regions, Study Suggests," *ScienceDaily*, October 21, 2011, accessed January 28, 2022, https://www.sciencedaily.com/releases/2011/10/111020025650.htm.

16. R. Kanai, B. Bahrami, R. Roylance, and G. Rees, "Online Social Network Size Is Reflected in Human Brain Structure," *Proceedings of the Royal Society B: Biological Sciences* 279, no. 1732 (2011): 1327–34, https://doi.org/10.1098/rspb.2011.1959.

17. Cleveland Clinic, "Why Multitasking Doesn't Work," March 10, 2021, accessed January 28, 2022, https://health.clevelandclinic.org/science-clear-multitasking-doesnt

-work/#:%7E:text=Multitasking%20can%20hinder%20your%20performance,likely%20to%20make%20a%20mistake.

18. J. A. Nielsen, B. A. Zielinski, M. A. Ferguson, J. E. Lainhart, and J. S. Anderson, "An Evaluation of the Left-Brain vs. Right-Brain Hypothesis with Resting State Functional Connectivity Magnetic Resonance Imaging," *PLoS ONE* 8, no. 8 (2013): e71275, https://doi.org/10.1371/journal.pone.0071275.

19. R. Pereira, vocalist and writer, "Hope, Faith, and Love," on *Going beyond the Stars*, Mumbai, India: Jesuit Music Ministry, 2001, compact disc.

CHAPTER 5

1. The Dhammapada, ch. 1, vv. 1–2 (New York: Oxford University Press, 1998).

2. P. Voss, M. E. Thomas, J. M. Cisneros-Franco, and T. de Villers-Sidani, "Dynamic Brains and the Changing Rules of Neuroplasticity: Implications for Learning and Recovery," *Frontiers in Psychology* 8 (2017), https://doi.org/10.3389/fpsyg.2017.01657.

3. S. L. Keng, M. J. Smoski, and C. J. Robins, "Effects of Mindfulness on Psychological Health: A Review of Empirical Studies," *Clinical Psychology Review* 31, no. 6 (2011): 1041–56, https://doi.org/10.1016/j.cpr.2011.04.006.

4. D. Vago, "The Effects of Meditation on Fibromyalgia," August 21, 2008, accessed January 28, 2022, https://davidvago.bwh.harvard.edu/the-effects-of-meditation-on-fibromyalgia/.

CHAPTER 6

1. R. Pereira, vocalist and writer, "The Challenge," on *Going beyond the Stars*, Mumbai, India: Jesuit Music Ministry, 2001, compact disc.

UNITING MIND, BODY, SPIRIT

2. R. Pereira, "The Challenge."
3. S. Begley, "The Brain: How the Brain Rewires Itself," TIME.com, January 19, 2007, http://content.time.com/time/magazine/article/0,9171,1580438,00.html.
4. R. Pereira, vocalist and writer, "Going beyond the Stars," on *Going beyond the Stars*, Mumbai, India: Jesuit Music Ministry, 2001, compact disc.

BIBLIOGRAPHY

Arias-Carrión, O., M. Stamelou, E. Murillo-Rodríguez, M. Menéndez-González, and E. Pöppel. "Dopaminergic Reward System: A Short Integrative Review." *International Archives of Medicine* 3 (2010): 24. https://doi.org/10.1186/1755-7682-3-24.

Beaty, R. E., P. Seli, and D. L. Schacter. "Thinking about the Past and Future in Daily Life: An Experience Sampling Study of Individual Differences in Mental Time Travel." *Psychological Research* 83, no. 4 (2018): 805–16. https://doi.org/10.1007/s00426-018-1075-7.

Begley, S. "The Brain: How the Brain Rewires Itself." TIME.com, January 19, 2007. http://content.time.com/time/magazine/article/0,9171,1580438,00.html.

Campbell, I. C. "Zoom Events Will Try to Re-create the In-person Conference Experience." The Verge. May 19, 2021. Accessed January 17, 2022. https://www.theverge.com/2021/5/19/22442919/zoom-live-events-paid-tickets-conferences-chat.

Centers for Disease Control and Prevention. "1918 Pandemic Influenza Historic Timeline." March 20, 2018. Accessed January 14, 2022. https://www.cdc.gov/flu/pandemic-resources/1918-commemoration/pandemic-timeline-1918.htm.

Cleveland Clinic. "Why Multitasking Doesn't Work." March 10, 2021. Accessed January 28, 2022. https://health.clevelandclinic.org/science-clear-multitasking-doesnt-work/

#:%7E:text=Multitasking%20can%20hinder%20your %20performance,likely%20to%20make%20a%20mistake.
Davidson, R. J., J. Kabat-Zinn, J. Schumacher, M. Rosenkranz, D. Muller, S. F. Santorelli, F. Urbanowski, A. Harrington, K. Bonus, and J. F. Sheridan. "Alterations in Brain and Immune Function Produced by Mindfulness Meditation." *Psychosomatic Medicine* 65, no. 4 (2003): 564–70. https://doi.org/10 .1097/01.psy.0000077505.67574.e3.
del Rio, C., and P. Malani. "COVID-19 in 2021—Continuing Uncertainty." *JAMA* 325, no. 14 (2021): 1389–90. https:// doi.org/10.1001/jama.2021.3760.
Desai, M. "Cryptocurrencies: The New Frontier." Financial Express. February 19, 2018. Accessed January 17, 2022. https://www.financialexpress.com/opinion/cryptocur rencies-the-new-frontier/1070967/.
Dhammapada. New York: Oxford University Press, 1998.
Frank, L. E., A. R. Preston, and D. Zeithamova. "Functional Connectivity between Memory and Reward Centers across Task and Rest Track Memory Sensitivity to Reward." *Cognitive, Affective and Behavioral Neuroscience* 19, no. 3 (2019): 503–22. https://doi.org/10.3758/s13415-019-00700-8.
Frederick, A. L., and G. D. Stanwood. "Drugs, Biogenic Amine Targets and the Developing Brain." *Developmental Neuroscience* 31, nos. 1–2 (2009): 7–22. https://doi.org/10.1159/ 000207490.
Goldsby, T. L., M. E. Goldsby, M. McWalters, and P. J. Mills. "Effects of Singing Bowl Sound Meditation on Mood, Tension, and Well-being: An Observational Study." *Journal of Evidence-Based Complementary and Alternative Medicine* 22, no. 3 (2016): 401–6. https://doi.org/10.1177/ 2156587216668109.
Grinyo, J. M. "Why Is Organ Transplantation Clinically Important?" *Cold Spring Harbor Perspectives in Medicine* 3, no.

6 (2013): a014985. https://doi.org/10.1101/cshperspect.a01 4985.

Harland, R., E. Antonova, G. S. Owen, M. Broome, S. Landau, Q. Deeley, and R. Murray. "A Study of Psychiatrists' Concepts of Mental Illness." *Psychological Medicine* 39, no. 6 (2008): 967–76. https://doi.org/10.1017/s0033291708004881.

Harris, J. "How the Internet Is Altering Your Mind." *The Guardian*, November 25, 2017. Accessed January 28, 2022. https://www.theguardian.com/technology/2010/aug/20/internet-altering-your-mind#:%7E:text=As%20Small%20put%20it%3A%20%22After,had%20already%20rewired%20their%20brains.%22.

He, D., S. Zhao, Y. Li, P. Cao, D. Gao, Y. Lou, and L. Yang. "Comparing COVID-19 and the 1918–19 Influenza Pandemics in the United Kingdom." *International Journal of Infectious Diseases* 98 (2020): 67–70. https://doi.org/10.1016/j.ijid.2020.06.075.

Kanai, R., B. Bahrami, R. Roylance, and G. Rees. "Online Social Network Size Is Reflected in Human Brain Structure." *Proceedings of the Royal Society B: Biological Sciences* 279, no. 1732 (2011): 1327–34. https://doi.org/10.1098/rspb.2011.1959.

Karch, C., C. Cruchaga, and A. Goate. "Alzheimer's Disease Genetics: From the Bench to the Clinic." *Neuron* 83, no. 1 (2014): 11–26. https://doi.org/10.1016/j.neuron.2014.05.041.

Keng, S. L., M. J. Smoski, and C. J. Robins. "Effects of Mindfulness on Psychological Health: A Review of Empirical Studies." *Clinical Psychology Review* 31, no. 6 (2011): 1041–56. https://doi.org/10.1016/j.cpr.2011.04.006.

Khantzian, E., and J. E. Mack. "Self-Preservation and the Care of the Self." *The Psychoanalytic Study of the Child* 38, no. 1 (1983): 209–32. https://doi.org/10.1080/00797308.1983.11823390.

Kumar, K., and S. Allarakha. "What Is the Normal Range for IQ?" MedicineNet, March 4, 2021b. Accessed January 28, 2022. https://www.medicinenet.com/what_is_the_normal_range_for_iq/article.htm.

Laskey, M. J. "A Cannonball Strike Kept Saint Ignatius Stuck in Bed. Thank God for That." Jesuits.Org. May 21, 2020. Accessed January 18, 2022. https://www.jesuits.org/stories/a-cannonball-strike-kept-saint-ignatius-stuck-in-bed-thank-god-for-that/.

Lee, Y. B., J. Yu, H. H. Choi, B. S. Jeon, H. K. Kim, S. W. Kim, S. S. Kim, Y. G. Park, and H. S. Chae. "The Association between Peptic Ulcer Diseases and Mental Health Problems." *Medicine* 96, no. 34 (2017): e7828. https://doi.org/10.1097/md.0000000000007828.

Loyola, I. O., and L. J. Puhl. *The Spiritual Exercises of St. Ignatius: Based on Studies in the Language of the Autograph.* 1st ed. Chicago: Loyola Press, 1968.

Maguire, E. A., K. Woollett, and H. J. Spiers. "London Taxi Drivers and Bus Drivers: A Structural MRI and Neuropsychological Analysis." *Hippocampus* 16, no. 12 (2006): 1091–101. https://doi.org/10.1002/hipo.20233.

McCarthy-Jones, C. T. S. U. S. "Are Social Networking Sites Controlling Your Mind?" *Scientific American*, December 8, 2017. Accessed January 28, 2022. https://www.scientificamerican.com/article/are-social-networking-sites-controlling-your-mind/.

McLellan, A. T. "Substance Misuse and Substance Use Disorders: Why Do They Matter in Healthcare?" *Transactions of the American Clinical and Climatological Association* 128 (2017): 112–30.

Meissner, W. W. *Ignatius of Loyola: The Psychology of a Saint.* New Haven, CT: Yale University Press, 1992.

Bibliography

Moncrieff, J., and D. Cohen. "How Do Psychiatric Drugs Work?" *BMJ* 338 (May 29, 2009): b1963. https://doi.org/10.1136/bmj.b1963.

Mosher, D. "High Wired: Does Addictive Internet Use Restructure the Brain?" *Scientific American*, June 17, 2011. Accessed January 28, 2022. https://www.scientificamerican.com/article/does-addictive-internet-use-restructure-brain/.

National Institute on Drug Abuse (NIDA). "Drugs and the Brain." July 27, 2021. Accessed January 25, 2022. https://www.drugabuse.gov/publications/drugs-brains-behavior-science-addiction/drugs-brain.

Nauert, C. G. "The Clash of Humanists and Scholastics: An Approach to Pre-Reformation Controversies." *Sixteenth Century Journal* 4, no. 1 (1973): 1–18. https://doi.org/10.2307/2539764.

Nielsen, J. A., B. A. Zielinski, M. A. Ferguson, J. E. Lainhart, and J. S. Anderson. "An Evaluation of the Left-Brain vs. Right-Brain Hypothesis with Resting State Functional Connectivity Magnetic Resonance Imaging." *PLoS ONE* 8, no. 8 (2013): e71275. https://doi.org/10.1371/journal.pone.0071275.

Pereira, R., vocalist and writer. "The Challenge." On *Going beyond the Stars*. Mumbai, India: Jesuit Music Ministry, 2001, compact disc.

———, vocalist and writer. "Going beyond the Stars." On *Going beyond the Stars*. Mumbai, India: Jesuit Music Ministry, 2001, compact disc.

———, vocalist and writer. "Hope, Faith, and Love." On *Going beyond the Stars*. Mumbai, India: Jesuit Music Ministry, 2001, compact disc.

———, "Meditation and Beyond: Phenomena Beyond Materialism." Paper presented at Cosmos, Nature and Culture: A Transdisciplinary Conference, Phoenix, AZ, July 2010.

Pereira, R., and J. Kozhamthadam. *The Human Soul in a World of the Neurological Sciences*. New Delhi: Indian Society for Promoting Christian Knowledge, 2021.

Pietrabissa, G., and S. G. Simpson. "Psychological Consequences of Social Isolation during COVID-19 Outbreak." *Frontiers in Psychology* 11 (2020). https://doi.org/10.3389/fpsyg.2020.02201.

Raab, D. "Calming the Monkey Mind: Do You Have an Inner Voice That Hinders Your Success? *Psychology Today*. September 13, 2017. Accessed January 22, 2022. https://www.psychologytoday.com/us/blog/the-empowerment-diary/201709/calming-the-monkey-mind.

Spreeuwenberg, P., M. Kroneman, and J. Paget. "Reassessing the Global Mortality Burden of the 1918 Influenza Pandemic." *American Journal of Epidemiology* 187, no. 12 (2018): 2561–67. https://doi.org/10.1093/aje/kwy191.

Srinahyanti, S., Y. Wau, I. Manurung, and N. Arjani, "Influence of Gadget: A Positive and Negative Impact of Smartphone Usage for Early Child." *Proceedings of the 2nd Annual Conference of Engineering and Implementation on Vocational Education (ACEIVE 2018), 3rd November 2018, North Sumatra, Indonesia*. EAI, 2019. https://doi.org/10.4108/eai.3-11-2018.2285692.

U.S. Department of Health and Human Services (HHS), Office of the Surgeon General. "Facing Addiction in America: The Surgeon General's Report on Alcohol, Drugs, and Health." Washington, DC: HHS, November 2016.

Vago, D. "The Effects of Meditation on Fibromyalgia." August 21, 2008. Accessed January 28, 2022. https://davidvago.bwh.harvard.edu/the-effects-of-meditation-on-fibromyalgia/.

Volkow, N. D., J. S. Fowler, G. J. Wang, and J. M. Swanson. "Dopamine in Drug Abuse and Addiction: Results from Imaging Studies and Treatment Implications." *Molecular Psychia-*

Bibliography

try 9, no. 6 (2004): 557–69. https://doi.org/10.1038/sj.mp.4001507.

Voss, P., M. E. Thomas, J. M. Cisneros-Franco, and T. de Villers-Sidani. "Dynamic Brains and the Changing Rules of Neuroplasticity: Implications for Learning and Recovery." *Frontiers in Psychology* 8 (2017). https://doi.org/10.3389/fpsyg.2017.01657.

Weinstein, A., L. Curtiss Feder, K. P. Rosenberg, and P. Dannon. "Internet Addiction Disorder." *Behavioral Addictions* (2014): 99–117. https://doi.org/10.1016/b978-0-12-407724-9.00005-7.

Wellcome Trust. "Number of Facebook Friends Linked to Size of Brain Regions, Study Suggests." *ScienceDaily*, October 21, 2011. Accessed January 28, 2022. https://www.sciencedaily.com/releases/2011/10/111020025650.htm.

Woollaston, V. "Generation Mobile Zombie: 1 in 10 Look at Their Phone As Soon As They Wake Up—And Almost 50% of People Check Their Mobile Phone at Least 50 Times a Day." DailyMail.com. September 8, 2015b. Accessed January 28, 2022. https://www.dailymail.co.uk/sciencetech/article-3226070/Generation-mobile-zombie-1-10-look-phone-soon-wake-50-check-50-times-day.html.

INDEX

addiction, 31–38, 41–44, 47
affirmation, 25, 65
awareness, ix, 11, 14–15, 18, 44, 49–50, 53–54, 57–58, 67

behavioral change, xvi–xviii, 12, 19–20, 34, 37–38, 43–45, 47, 54, 70
belief, 47, 51, 65, 66
breathing, 12, 15, 17–18, 57

cannonball, 5–6
chemical, 10, 31–32, 39, 43, 51
climate change, xvii, 2, 46
concentration, 14, 17, 59
confirmation, 23–25, 27, 29, 30
consciousness, 54
consolation, 22, 67
context, xvii, 36, 60–62, 65

desire, ix, xvii, 7, 25, 29, 33, 70

discernment, xvi–xvii, 19, 21–24, 26–28, 56, 70
dopamine, 33, 44

emotion, 4, 9, 12, 22, 33–34, 40, 53–54
equity, 56
examen, 67
examination of consciousness, 66–67
exercise, 10, 16, 19, 41, 42, 48, 56–58, 67

faith, vii, ix, xi, xii, 4, 6, 21, 23, 25, 27, 30, 42, 43, 46, 47
focusing, 14, 15, 17, 18, 49, 58
freedom, xvii, 11, 43, 44, 47, 55, 62–64

goal, xi, 7, 20, 22, 23, 38, 45–47, 49, 57, 62
gratitude, xvii, 66, 67

happiness, xvii, xviii, 70
hope, x, 2, 6, 8, 9, 27, 42, 43, 46, 53
human flourishing, xvii, 9, 11, 49, 55

Ignatius, vii, x, xv–xvii, 5–9, 18–22, 24–26, 50, 62, 67, 68, 70
immune system, xvii, 52, 54

love, xii, 4, 7, 17, 20, 26, 41–43, 53, 63–65

Magis, xvii, 68
meditation, 14–18, 25, 49, 56, 57, 59, 67, 68
memory, 13, 34, 36–39
mindfulness, vii, x, xv, xvii, 47–50, 53–59, 66, 68

mission, xvii, 6, 7, 29, 68
multitasking, 40, 41
music, x, xiv, 4, 41, 65, 66

neuroscience, xi, xii, xvi, xvii, 11, 19, 32, 44, 49, 50, 66, 70
nonsubstance, 34, 36, 38

positive attitude, ix, 46
psychosomatic illness, 13
purpose, xvii, xviii, 22

repetition, 13, 19, 50

serotonin, 32, 44
stress, x, 12, 13, 14, 20

willpower, 44, 55

Zoom, xv, xvi, 2–5, 62

ABOUT THE AUTHOR

Fr. Roy loves teaching and sharing with people all that he learns. He comes from a family of teachers, starting with his mom. He has master's degrees in chemistry, theology, and philosophy, with a PhD from Boston College in the interdisciplinary areas of chemistry, neuroscience, and consciousness. He has taught chemistry, neuroscience, biomedical ethics, medical humanities, philosophy, theology, piano, singing, jiving, swimming, yoga, meditation, personality development, value education, acting, public speaking, and even cooking. Working in educational institutions during the week and celebrating Mass or hiking and camping with students during the weekend keep him busy. Most of all he loves people and is happy to offer whatever tips he has picked up to those interested in loving life and living fully. Celebrating the Eucharist brings him joy because it is an expression of his ordination motto, "To experience God and help others experience God," which he has tried to live out for the past twenty-five years.

Fr. Roy Pereira is the Special Assistant to the Senior Vice President of Student Affairs in charge of Wellness at Loyola Marymount University, Los Angeles. Previously, he taught in the School of Medicine at Creighton University. Prior to arriving at Creighton, he was Vice-Principal (Academics) and Head, Department of Chemistry, at St. Xavier's College (Autonomous), Mumbai, for over two decades. One aspect of his research covers the effects of cell phones, internet usage, and social media on the brain, for which he was invited by Google Headquarters, Mountain

UNITING MIND, BODY, SPIRIT

View, California, to speak to their employees. His research also involves the understanding of the mind-body link, the effect of meditation on health outcomes, the placebo effect, neurofeedback, and ways of dealing with stress in our lives. He was invited by Harvard University to speak on the topic "Mind-Body Connection" at a conference. His most recent coedited book, *The Human Soul in a World of the Neurological Sciences* is now available on Amazon.

He has been invited to speak on various topics in the United States, Canada, the United Kingdom, Germany, Singapore, Australia, and New Zealand, including doing a TEDx talk. His presentations are interactive, and he strives to explain complex concepts from neuroscience in easy-to-understand ways using multimedia, music, and the piano. He has a sizeable presence on YouTube with a mix of videos on academic matters as well as music, including his own compositions.

For any queries, suggestions, or speaker engagements, feel free to drop an email to either pereiraroy2005@gmail.com or Roy.Pereira@lmu.edu.